THE DOMESDAY BOOK OF
GIANT SALMON
VOLUME II

THE DOMESDAY BOOK OF
GIANT SALMON
VOLUME II

More Records of the Largest Atlantic Salmon Ever Caught

Fred Buller

CONSTABLE

For my lady – Margaret

First published by Constable, an imprint of
Constable & Robinson Ltd
3 The Lanchesters
162 Fulham Palace Road
London W6 9ER
www.constablerobinson.com

Copyright © Fred Buller 2010
Maps: William Smuts

The right of Fred Buller to be identified as the author of this work has been asserted by him in accordance with the Copyright, Designs and Patents Act, 1988.

All rights reserved. This book is sold subject to the condition that it shall not, by way of trade or otherwise, be lent, re-sold, hired out or otherwise circulated in any form other than that in which it is published and without a similar condition including this condition being imposed on the subsequent purchaser.

A copy of the British Library Cataloguing in Publication Data is available from the British Library.

ISBN: 978 1 84901 387 1

Printed and bound in China

PREVIOUS PAGE: *In autumn 2007, Norway's newspaper* Altenposten *published this photograph of a male salmon weighing 60lb 12oz. It weighed 67lb when it was originally netted from the Alten river. The fish was 54¾in long, and the largest male salmon ever used at the Alta Hatchery to fertilize eggs from a large hen fish.*

CONTENTS

Acknowledgements 6
Foreword 8
Introduction 10

THE LISTS
List 1   Salmon over 50lb caught on fly 13
List 2   Salmon between 50 and 60lb method uncertain 19
List 3   Salmon over 60lb caught by any method 23

Maps 27

SALMON OVER 50LB CAUGHT ON FLY 31
SALMON BETWEEN 50 AND 60LB METHOD UNCERTAIN 85
SALMON OVER 60LB CAUGHT BY ANY METHOD 97

ADDENDA TO VOLUME I 129

NOT STRICTLY SPEAKING . . . 185

APPENDICES 199

Bibliography 228
Picture Credits 229
Index 230

ACKNOWLEDGEMENTS

The *Domesday Book of Giant Salmon, A Record of the Largest Atlantic Salmon Ever Caught*, was first published in Britain in 2007 and reprinted a year later with four extra entries. At the same time, a reprint with a different title, more suited to the North American market, was published in Canada and the USA by Firefly Books Ltd. Now this second volume features eighty-four new entries, including the four from the reprint – so as to keep the purchasers of the first edition, like the purchasers of the reprint, fully informed – while the addenda also provide more information on some previous entries and the appendices include background studies that may interest readers. The final stages of putting a book together while new material is arriving in a steady flow, as it was with the first volume, is usually a bit fraught. Although a number of late entries were acknowledged in the appendices, the catch details were not given in the lists. Accordingly, the details of eleven new entries from Sweden that were noticed in Appendix 3 have now been added to the lists.

ACKNOWLEDGEMENTS

The fact that I have so much new material at my disposal is mainly due to an astonishing response by readers from all over Europe, North America and even South Africa. Indeed, the fulfilling task of exchanging letters with correspondents who happened to know the answers to so many puzzles, or who had details of a catch that had previously escaped my attention, has made me exceedingly grateful to them. I would like to thank in particular Mr Flitcroft, who received Steve McPadden's letter concerning Mr Myran's Nid River salmon and passed it on to me – such is the way that important documentation is gradually assembled; John Tiddy of St Ives, who sent me the copy of *Trout & Salmon* containing the story of Donald Parrish's big Wye salmon; and angling correspondent Colin Bradshaw for information regarding Ragnor Tenvik's 54½lb Namsen River salmon. I am also grateful to Grail Priddice, for permission to use the cutting relating to the 60lb salmon netted in the Moray Firth; to Morten Harangen for locating Fridgeir Sagmo's descendents and to Fridgeir's daughter for permission to publish the photograph of his salmon; and to Anthony Desbruslais, the owner of the oil painting of the 76¼lb River Dee salmon.

Although I am not savvy with modern methods of communication, I do have a friend who is – his name is David Hatwell. I would like to thank him again for the considerable help he has given me, not least in the ongoing work of archiving the approximately 5,000 letters written by or to me since 1943. I would also like to thank Dr Roy Flury, who scrutinized the manuscript – especially those parts that are devoted to Scandinavia – with the eyes of a raptor. Finally, I would like to thank Kay Varney and Marion Paull – ladies whose behind-the-scenes assistance in working the machinery (typing and editing) that translates thoughts into print has been vital to the production of my books.

Fred Buller
February 2010

FOREWORD

The publication of *The Domesday Book of Giant Salmon*, the first volume, in October 2007, marked a celebration both for salmon fishing and the salmon themselves. The fishermen had taken many of the books off the publisher's shelves by Christmas and the salmon it seemed came to the party when they returned from the sea the following spring. On the River Alten at least the 2008 run of large salmon was astonishing. No fewer than nine fish weighing 50 pounds or more and three of 49 pounds were taken on rod and line during the season. And the icing on the cake was an 82 pound fish taken in the nets in Altenfjord.

Since the book was published, Buller has received a steady stream of letters and telephone calls from around the world. Some of these were congratulatory, others gave information on big fish not mentioned in the book and some noted corrections or gave other details on the listed fish. And so in just a few months, a second volume of *The Domesday Book of Giant Salmon* was conceived. It is now presented in a format to match the first volume.

The success of the first volume was, I believe, due as much to the clarity and inspiration of Buller's writing as it was to the size of the fish. Thanks to this the book is simply an exceptional read. I have enjoyed, on occasions, the privilege of sitting with Fred in his study and discussing some of his letters and reports – an experience not to be missed. He does not admit it, but I feel he enjoys the muddled yet promising reports more than the others. However long it takes, sometimes many months, he just loves the investigation, the chase. He may no longer come out of the trap like a greyhound hell-bent on catching the hare, but perhaps he is more the bloodhound, ears cocked, tail wagging, taking his time, but always getting his man!

I do sincerely thank Fred for inviting me one day, some five years ago, to read the manuscript of *Volume I*. It has been a truly fascinating journey. This book, *The Domesday Book of Giant Salmon, Volume II*, will be Buller's ninth on angling subjects. These books cover a time span from Dame Juliana in 1496 to a salmon caught in 2009. A remarkable man – a very remarkable man.

Roy Flury
Oxford
June 2010

Dame Juliana Berners is the supposed author of The Book of Hawking, Hunting, and Blasing of Arms, *also known as* The Book of St Albans, *published in the fifteenth century, which contains a verse treatise on 'the manere of huntynge for all manere of bestys'.*

INTRODUCTION

Very few salmon fishermen ever manage to catch a salmon weighing over 50lb on fly. For this reason, such fish are the subject of List 1, in this volume as in the first. In Volume I this list comprised 170 entries, to which Volume II adds an additional forty-six new entries. However, such a list can only be tentative because so many 50-pounders have been documented without mention of the method used to catch them. List 2, therefore, labelled 'method uncertain', contains fish weighing between 50 and 60lb that *may* have been caught on fly. There were no fewer than 146 fish in this rod-caught category in Volume I, and there are seventeen new entries in Volume II. As in the first volume, this list does not contain any fish from North America, perhaps because of the almost exclusive use of fly-fishing for Atlantic Salmon there. I have not explored the catch records of fish between 50lb and 60lb caught on bait simply because their numbers would have made the task of compiling such a list impossibly large.

Salmon of 60lb are so exceptionally rare that they have been recorded in a third list which disregards the method used for their capture. List 3 in Volume I contains 152 of the largest Atlantic Salmon ever caught. The corresponding list in this volume contains twenty-one additional entries. It is unlikely that many fish of such a weight have escaped attention unless they were caught in saltwater or in the River Rhine, before pollution and netting ruined it as a salmon fishery.

As in the first volume, for each fish there may have been several sources of information, and corroboration. The sources cited in the lists are generally the first that I have come across; others may be detailed in the relevant stories that follow.

In the UK, weights used to be recorded using the Dutch system of pounds, but the 1826 Imperial Weights and Measures Act brought in the current avoirdupois system throughout Britain. Dutch pounds may be converted to English pounds by dividing by 1,085 – this has been mentioned wherever relevant in the accounts of the big fish.

Detailed records of the many large fish caught in Norway, especially on the biggest rivers, such at the Alten (also known as the Alta), Namsen, Tana and Vosso are few and far between. However, it is possible to come across old photographs and wooden models of the fish. Such photographs often show a fisherman holding a long fly rod with a large reel at the butt end, which suggests the angler was fly-fishing, but it does not necessarily mean that he or she was *casting* a fly as the angler may have been harling with a fly, and even using a small spinner or fly spoon.

According to John Ashley-Cooper, most big salmon caught in Scottish rivers before 1900 would have been caught on fly, although some fish may have been caught harling with fly, especially those caught on the Tay. I have included as many stories of the capture of the giant salmon listed as he has been able to find.

I have not included, in either volume, many of the very large salmon that have been caught and released without being weighed in recent years, despite some of these being supported by photographs and plausible estimates. As both volumes reveal, photographs are a hopelessly unreliable means of estimating size, and it is difficult if not impossible to estimate the weight of a fish from hastily gathered information about length and girth. Although attempts have been made to equip boatmen, both in Norway and in Britain, with special lightweight weighing nets and accurate spring balances to weigh fish before releasing them, such efforts have often proved impractical. Essentially it is almost impossible to put a credible weight to a fish that has been released which is acceptable from the point of view of keeping records.

An 1849 watercolour by Scottish artist J.F. Campbell depicting the 'first' Sandia camp on the River Alten in Norway at dinner time on a washing day.

LIST 1
SALMON OVER 50lb
CAUGHT ON FLY

No.	Weight lb oz	Length (in)	Girth (in)	Location	Country	Captor
1	49 8	48	30	Vosso River	Norway	Terry Golding
2	50			River Esk	Scotland	Unknown
3	50			Bervie Bay	Scotland	Provost John Burness
4	50			Alten River	Norway	Stian Hammersvik
5	50 8			Grand Cascapedia	Canada	Dr Drummond
6	50 8			Morrum River	Sweden	P. Bjorklund
7	50 12			Alten River	Norway	Paul Inge Thomassen
8	50 12	52		Orkla River	Norway	Heiki Kemppainen
9	51	50	34	Alten River	Norway	Shirley Deterding
10	51	50	32	Alten River	Norway	Sir David Hoare
11	51			Alten River	Norway	David Clarke
12	51			Alten River	Norway	Morton Seaman
13	51 6			Morrum River	Sweden	R. Johnsson
14	51 8			Alten River	Norway	James Greenwood
15	51 12			Alten River	Norway	Thorieif Hammari
16	51 14			Morrum River	Sweden	O. Andreasson
17	52			Alten River	Norway	Morton Seaman
18	52	48		River Tay	Scotland	Major Cunard
19	52			Alten River	Norway	John McMillan
20	52 8	50	27	Alten River	Norway	Charles Balbach
21	52 10			Alten River	Norway	Rupert Lea
22	52 10			Morrum River	Sweden	Unknown
23	52 11½			Repparfjord River	Norway	Tor Johnny Sivertsen
24	53			Vefsen River	Norway	Unknown
25	53			Alten River	Norway	Willy Thomassen
26	53 3			Morrum River	Sweden	C. Palm
27	53 8			Namsen River	Norway	Miss E.Spiller
28	53 10			River Em	Sweden	J. Derelhad
29	53 12			River Em	Sweden	L.P. Gustafsson
30	54			River Mersey	England	Unknown
31	54			Namsen River	Norway	A. Park
32	54			Alten River	Norway	Einar Antonsen

Date	Beat	Source
June 1991		*Trout & Salmon*, August 1991
1889		*The Salmon*, edited by A.E. Gathorne-Hardy (1898)
1937		Letter from Derek Mills
August 2007	Bollo Pool	Personal communication from Stian Hammersvik to David Hatwell
1890		*Outing* magazine, December 1890
22 June 1991		Anders Sorensson's List
18 June 2008		Correspondence with Sir Edward Dashwood Bt
August 2008		*Altaposten* newspaper, 2008
August 2006	Langstilla	David Hatwell and personal communication
July 2007	Snoski	Personal communication
13 July 2009	Rich Holda	Courtesy of the Alta Association
11 July 1992	Nedre Sierra	Courtesy of the Alta Association
26 April 1992		Anders Sorensson's List
5 July 2008	Langstilla	Direct correspondence
2007		Norwegian website
29 September 1993		Anders Sorensson's List
9 July 1994	Langstilla	Courtesy of the Alta Association
1907		Cased fish in Wheatsheaf Inn, Egton, Yorkshire
2008	Sandiagoski	Ivar Leinan via Dr Roy Flury
2008	Bollo Pool	Ivar Leinen via Dr Roy Flury
9 July 2008	Snoski	Correspondence with James Greenwood
10 May 2000		*This Fishing Life*, Bob Church (2003)
10 July 2009	Josefsens Pool	www.fishing-norway.com
c1900	Foss Pool	*Fishing Country Life* (1904), p.228
7 August 1995	Ovre-Sorrisniva	Communication from David Hatwell
13 July 1992		Anders Sorensson's List
1903	Grande	*Fishing Country Life* (1904)
5 October 1992	Home Pool	Goran Ulfsparre's List
2 May 2000	Sea Pool	Goran Ulfsparre's List
1763	Latchford Causey	*The Art of Angling*, Richard Brookes (1774). Brookes says the fish was caught on fly, perhaps.
1902	Selloeg	*Fishing Country Life* (1904)
1 July 2000	Midterfaret	Communication from David Hatwell

No.	Weight lb oz	Length (in)	Girth (in)	Location	Country	Captor
33	54	46	28	Alten River	Norway	Mollie Fitzgerald
34	54 3			River Em	Sweden	L. Postonen
35	54 7			Morrum River	Sweden	M. Bjorkman
36	55			Bardo/Malang	Norway	An English tenant
37	55			North Esk River	Scotland	A relation of Patrick Chalmers
38	55	50	32	Alten River	Norway	Richard Onslow
39	55 6			Morrum River	Sweden	E. Nedergaar
40	56			Alten River	Norway	Jeremy Bloch
41	57 6	54	29 7/8	Alten River	Norway	Ernst Daniloff
42	58			Namsen River	Norway	Boatman
43	58 6			Surna River	Norway	John H. Dalsegg
44	58 13			Morrum River	Sweden	P. Brugmann
45	58 13½	54	27	Alten River	Norway	Ulf-Arne Jungord Nilsen
46	58 9½	52½	29½	Em River	Sweden	Holger Lauth

Date	Beat	Source
June 2008	Lower Sierra	Personal communication
29 September 1992	Sea Pool	Goran Ulfsparre's List
27 May 1992		Anders Sorensson's List
c.1893		*My Sporting Life*, John Waller Hills (1936)
October 1925		*Where the Spring Salmon Run* Patrick E. Chalmers (1931)
8 July 2006	Lower Dango	Direct communication
26 July 1994		Anders Sorensson's List
July 2008	Vina Gorva	Letter from Bozo Ivanovic
July 2007	Langstilla Pool	Courtesy of www.finmarkdagblad.no
1902	Vibstad	*Fishing Country Life* (1904)
1922		Personal communication with Morten Harangen
31 May 1992		Anders Sorensson's List
August 2008	Farm Mikkeli	*Altaposten* newspaper, 17 August 2008
2008	Blackwater Pool	Personal communication from Marcus Weyerke

This watercolour, painted in 1849 by J.F. Campbell, shows boats being dragged at the Gilvo rapids, then known as the Sara rapids, on the River Alten.

LIST 2
SALMON BETWEEN 50 AND 60lb
METHOD UNCERTAIN

No.	Weight lb oz	Length (in)	Girth (in)	Location	Country	Captor
47	50			Loch Tay	Scotland	Unknown
48	50			River Dee	Wales	Unknown
49	50			River Vefsen	Norway	Joyce Farrer
50	51			River Blackwater	Ireland	Unknown
51	51 8			Cumberland Derwent	England	Dr A. Peck
52	51 8			Namsen River	Norway	Lt Col N.G. Pearson
53	52			River Dee	Wales	Unknown
54	52			Namsen River	Norway	Lt Col N.G. Pearson
55	52			Namsen River	Norway	Sir Charles Blois
56	53	52½	30	Hampshire Avon	England	Unknown
57	53 8			River Tweed	Scotland	Unknown
58	54	52		Grimsey	Iceland	Unknown
59	54 8	52	29	Namsen River	Norway	Mrs Williams
60	54 9			Namsen River	Norway	Karl Greiff Olsen
61	56 4			Namsen River	Norway	Mr Gibson
62	57 6			Namsen River	Norway	Oddgeir Brumo
63	58 6		30	Nid River	Norway	Mr Myran

Date	Beat	Source
1880		*The Natural History of British Fishes*, Frank Buckland (1881)
1899	Llandrino	*Angling*, Oct/Dec 1940; rod caught
1934	Föisjord	Correspondence with Trevor Farrer (son)
1890		*Fishing Gazette*, 1 March 1890
1872		*The Salmon*, edited by A.E. Gathorne-Hardy (1898), March 2008
9 July 1932	Kariol Pool	Personal communication with the Rev. Nigel Pearson
1779	Pickhill	*Angling*, Oct/Dec 1940; rod caught
9 July 1930	Kariol Pool	Personal communication with the Rev. Nigel Pearson
pre. 1864	Fiskum Foss	*By Lake and River*, Francis Francis (1874)
2 April 1880		*The Natural History of British Fishes*, Frank Buckland (1881)
1873		*The Salmon*, edited by A.E. Gathorne Hardy (1898)
1957		Letters from Dr Derek Mills and Arnie Isaksson
1928	Gartland	Personal communication with the Rev. Nigel Pearson
June 1962	Overhalla	*Namsen I Våre Minner* 1985
26 June 1957		*Namsen I Våre Minner* 1985
15 June 1951		*Namsen I Våre Minner* 1985
1916		Per Oyvind Myran

'Staking up to Sandia' on the River Alten, painted by J.F. Campbell.

LIST 3
SALMON OVER 60lb
CAUGHT BY ANY METHOD

No.	Weight lb	oz	Length (in)	Girth (in)	Location	Country	Captor
64	60				River Wye	England	J. Evans
65	60		54	30	Moray Firth	Scotland	Hugh Cameron
66	60		54	24	Severn	Wales	Killed by an otter
67	60	14	50¾	31½	Eids River	Norway	Martin Hjelle
68	62				Border Esk	England	Mr Johnstone
69	62	14			Namsen River	Norway	Mrs Curtis
70	63		55	29	The North Esk	Scotland	Netsmen
71	65				Unknown	Norway	Unknown
72	66	2			Namsen River	Norway	Fridgeir Sagmo
73	68	8			Firth of Forth	Scotland	Netsmen
74	69				River Rhine	Germany	Unknown netsman
75	70				River Thames	England	Unknown
76	70	8			Faroese waters	Faroes	Professional long-liners
77	71	6	52¾	33	Suldal River	Norway	Netsmen
78	72	8			River Thames	England	The Coxens
79	72	12	56¼	31¾	Suldal River	Norway	Netsmen
80	75				Sand River	Norway	Mr Grieg
81	76	4			River Dee	Unknown	Unknown
82	82	10			Alten Fjord	Norway	Egil Olai Bårdsen & Dagfinn Nic
83	102	8			Nemen River	Lithuania	Netsmen
84	109				River Hope	Scotland	Poacher

LIST 3 – SALMON OVER 60LB CAUGHT BY ANY METHOD

Date	Beat	Source
c.1850		*Angler's Companion to the Rivers and Lochs of Scotland*, Stoddart
July 1856		*Inverness Advertiser*, 15 July 1856
1889		*Fishing Gazette*, 4 January 1890
May 1944	Eidselva	Dr Marcus Weyerke
1902	Kirk Andrews	*Cumberland News*
1938	Verium	*Namsen I Våre Minner* 1985
June 1890		*Fishing Gazette*, 21 June 1899
		Fishing Gazette, 8 June 1907
28 May 1931	Reve	*Namsen I Våre Minner* 1985
1871		Personal communication with Hugh Newton
		So We Fished on the Lower Rhine, Werner Bocking (1989)
1789		*Fishing: Salmon And Trout*, H. Cholmondeley-Pennell (1885)
1982		Personal communication with Derek Mills
1952		Letter from Sir Edward Dashwood Bt
1820	Twickenham	*Fishing Gazette*, 6 July 1883
1947		Letter from Sir Edward Dashwood Bt
1913		Letter to Lew Watts from Lief Inge Andersen
1875		Personal communication with Anthony Desbruslais
July 2008		*Altaposten* newspaper, 5 July 2008
		www.worldrecords.com/salmon
Sept 1960		Personal communication with Dr Paul Riley

The Blackwater at Lismore Castle.

MAPS

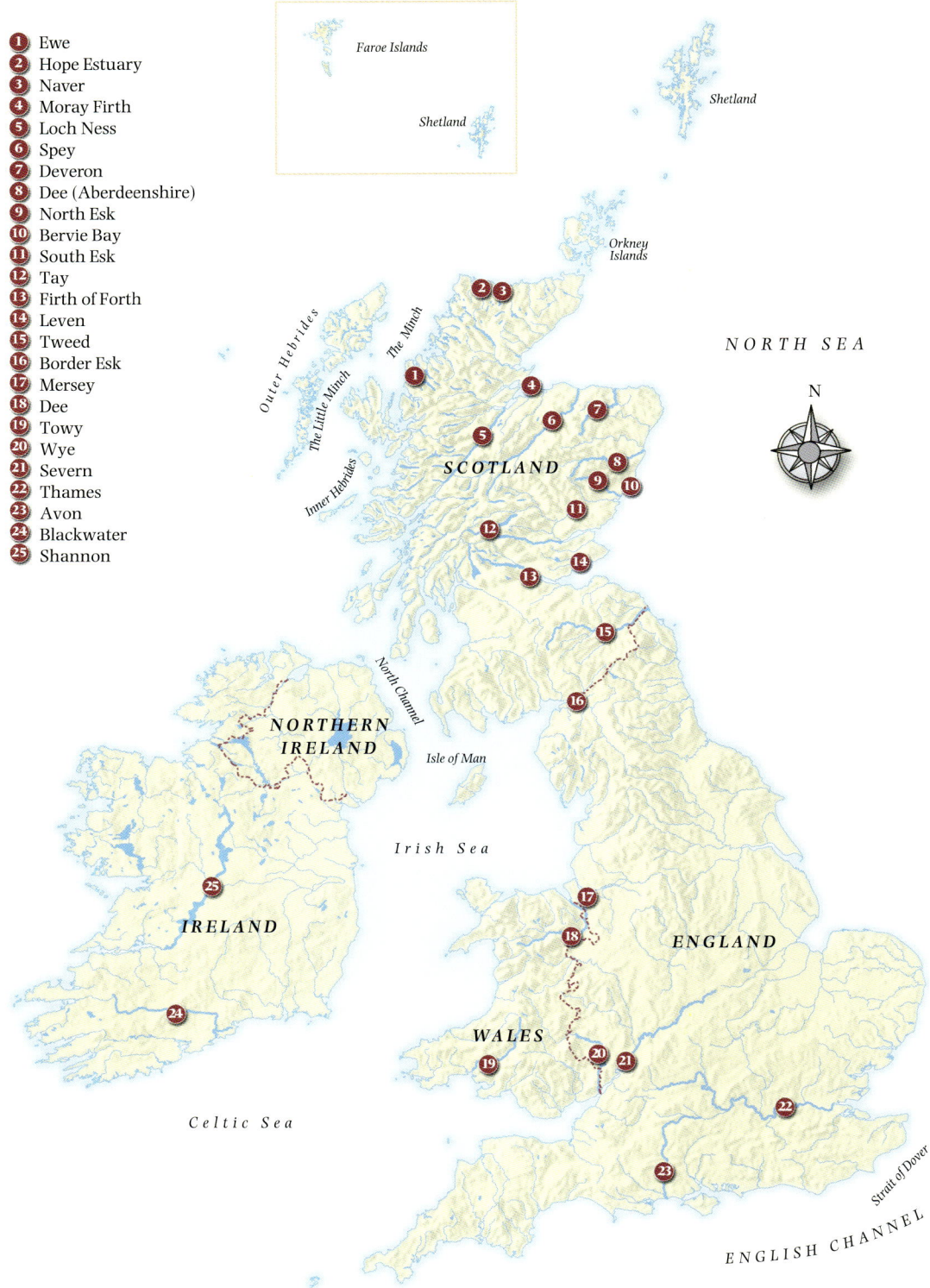

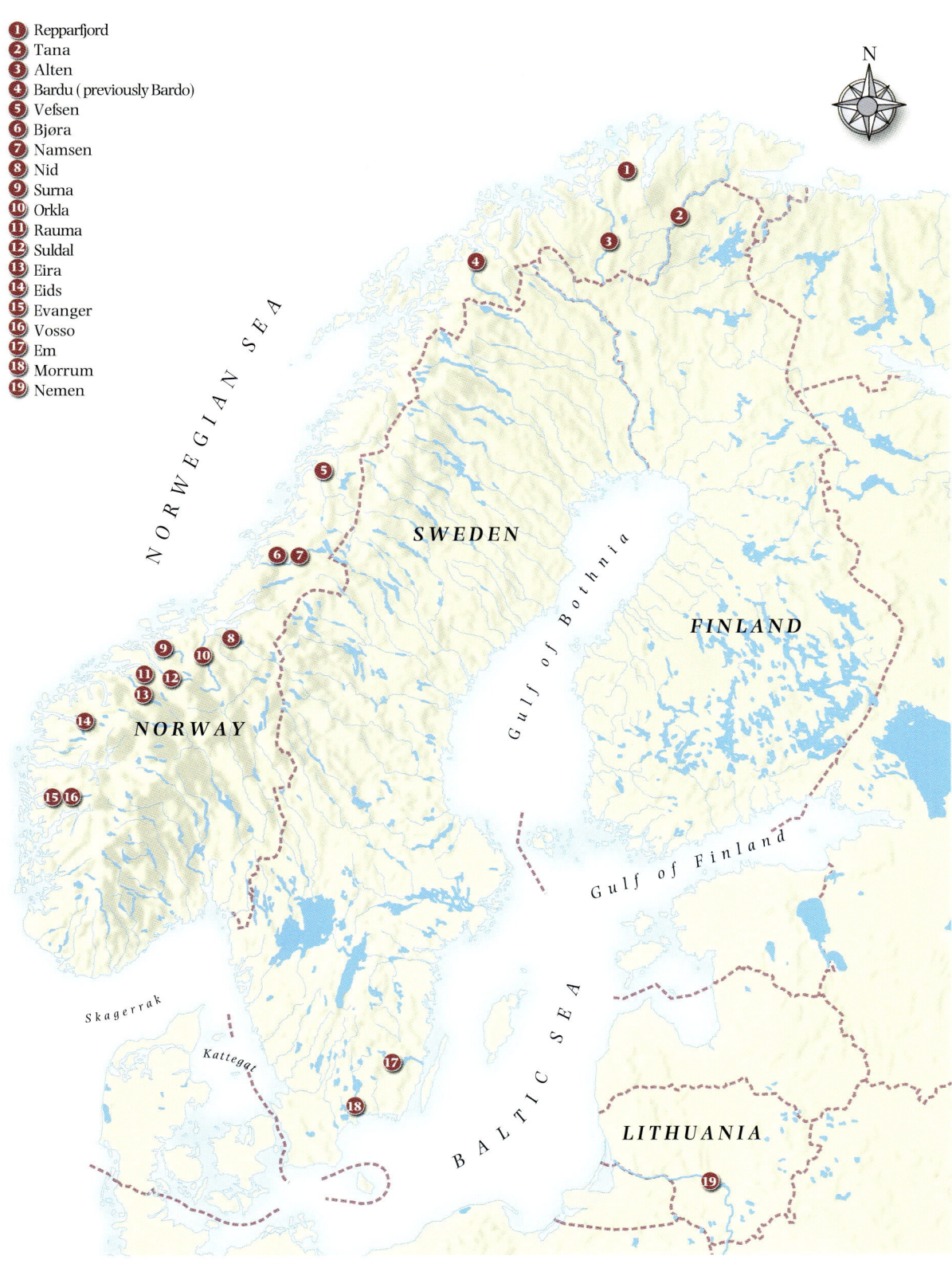

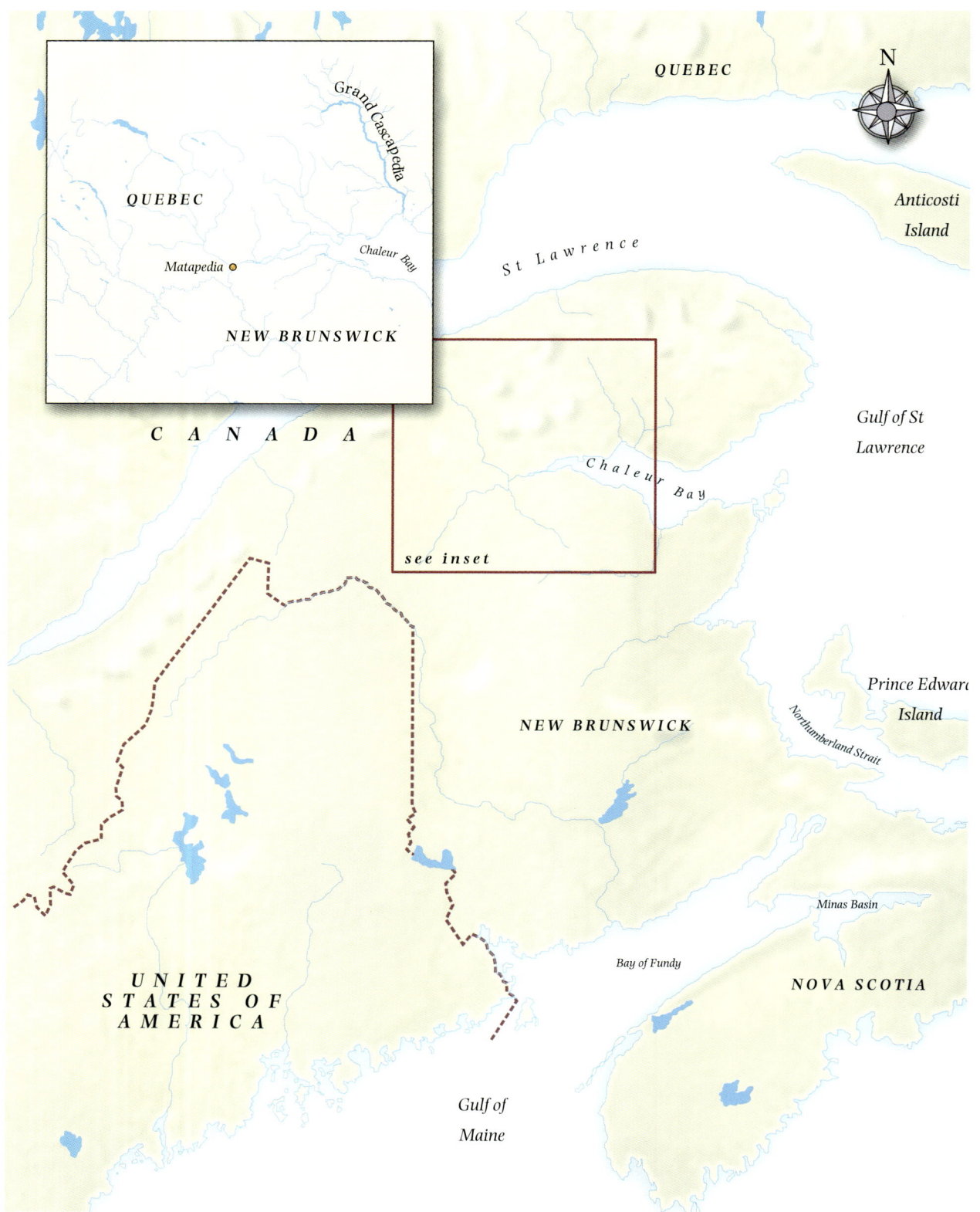

SALMON OVER 50lb CAUGHT ON FLY

TERRY GOLDING'S VOSSO RIVER SALMON
—— No. 1 ——

Rod-caught 50lb salmon are rare – so rare in fact that the publishing of this book utterly depends on their scarcity. But, if you closely study all the reports of monster salmon, you will find that the rarest of them all is one weighing 49½lb. I know someone who caught such a fish and his name is Terry Golding. I didn't include his salmon in the first edition, although I knew all about it, for the simple reason that to justify the title of *Giant Salmon* I needed to have a qualifying weight that was startling and so dream-like as to be almost unattainable – so I fixed on 50lb. Moreover, a fish would only be included if it was caught on fly (my starting weight for fish caught by other methods was 60lb).

My justification for restricting the number of entries was to ensure that the material collected would ultimately make a nice bulky book but not so bulky as to demand a two-volume edition. However, the strictness of my plan came to grief when I included Miss Davey's 59½lb Wye salmon (No. 318), which fell to a spinner.

A glance at Mr Golding's salmon reveals its perfect condition and shape, and the photograph of the captor and his fish is very impressive – photographing fishermen with a big fish may appear to be a simple task but, in reality, it is notoriously difficult. This picture is surpassed only by the photograph of Morton Seaman with his 52-pounder.

If the following account doesn't give you the desire to fish for salmon in Norway, nothing will. It is extracted from Terry Golding's original, which was published in *Trout & Salmon* in August 1991 and illustrated with eight of Roger Hughes's photographs.

On 1 June that year, on the opening day of the season on Norway's Vosso river, Terry Golding was fishing on the Oyne beat:

> When I first went to fish the Vosso I viewed with some trepidation a trip down the rapids that separate one pool from another. But after six years of watching friends careering down the rapids in hot pursuit of glass-case salmon I was now beginning to feel disappointed that I had not had a fish large enough to force me to do the same.
>
> At 10.35 a.m., with the fly [a two-inch black and yellow tube with a size 4 treble] almost on the dangle, I had a solid pull and was into a fish. As salmon often do in the early stages of a fight, the fish came in towards the boat and seemed content merely to swim backwards and forwards while

Terry Golding pictured with his magnificent Vosso salmon. How lucky he was to have had a series of superb photographs taken by Roger Hughes. In my opinion, the photographs are so good that Hughes should be elevated to the rank of cameraman.

I heaved on the rod. Even at that stage it seemed like a good fish, and I did begin to wonder whether at last I was about to reach my 'holy grail' of a 30lb salmon.

By a stroke of good luck, Roger Hughes had been fishing the Bridge Pool below us with David Hodgkiss, one of the owners of the fishing. He had seen the rod bend almost at the minute the fish took, had hurried up to Oyne complete with camera, and was now reclining on a grassy bank taking pictures and chatting to the gillie [Brian Palmer], who by now had worked the boat into a backwater where I thought I might be able to land the fish. The fish, however, had other ideas, and the sheer power of his runs was already making my arm ache. Brian, with classic understatement, said he did not think we were going to end the battle in Oyne. The fish must have overheard, because with one almighty run he was over to the far side of the river and into the fierce current.

'We're going to have to go down,' said Brian, and I vaguely recall wondering how frightened I was going to be – but there was no time for that. Here was the fish of a lifetime running 50 yards away in an unstoppable rush and the only thing I could concentrate on was staying in touch with him. As we entered the rapids, I tried to get as much line back on the reel as quickly as I could. I remember thinking there was no point worrying about the boat or where we were going with it. That was Brian's job, and I had no choice but to put my complete faith in his abilities.

I was now playing the fish in the Bridge Pool and, some 30 minutes after the battle had commenced, we had neither seen him nor had any sign that he was the least bit tired. Again, I thought we might just be landing the fish in this pool – especially as the boat had been rowed close in to the bank – but now the fish was off again and we were into the rapids and following the fish under the famous Bolstadoyri Bridge.

After a further 15 minutes of shenanigans, the boat's occupants pulled up to the bank for the third time in the hope that they were going to make their stand, but alas that was not the case.

There was absolutely no sign that he was any less fresh than when I hooked him. To prove the point, the fish made a heart-stopping run right across the river. The fish was now heading downstream and if he tried to go down into the fjord, we would be in all sorts of trouble. The final set of rapids at this water height made the previous sets look like a millpond. There was only

As they go down the rapids, Brian Palmer holds the boat on the oars so as to retain the pressure exerted on the fish – no more and no less.

one possible way down and that was on the far side, where the current was not quite so fierce. This meant that we first had to get across the river at the very part where the stream starts to build up its greatest force.

By the time we followed the salmon down into the fjord I was again wondering where my fish was. When I finally got the line back on the reel, the fish was not in the calm waters of the fjord but right in the middle of the most terrifying rapids and heading back up them! This was unbelievable!

For a few minutes I actually thought he was going back up to the lower Bridge Pool but then in another electrifying run he was back downstream and out into the fjord. Here was our chance. In the quieter water perhaps we could tow him around a bit, or at least lead him in to the bank. So here I was again, beached on a shingle bank.

Brian was out of the boat and in the water with his gaff at the ready. This was it – and as I reeled in still further, we saw our fish for the first time. Unfortunately, the fish saw us, too, took off again like a torpedo and forced us back into the boat to give chase in the fjord.

If the fish was exhausted, as I now began foolishly to hope, I would never be able to drag him up from the depths with the tackle I was using.

My mouth was dry and Brian confirmed that he had the same trouble. The sheer tension and physical effort had affected us equally. I was now absolutely exhausted. I was dropping the rod, and my reel-winding hand had seized up. 'Couldn't you row nearer the fish,' I remember asking Brian, 'and perhaps gaff him into the boat?' This was desperation indeed, but a curt, 'No way,' told me that I would have to keep going.

When Brian eventually beached the boat, we were on the far side of the fjord and as I started painfully to reel the fish in, he saw us again and would not come in to the shallower water over a shingle bank. I heaved as hard as I could and tried to steer him to the gaff. Brian had gone in almost to his waist to assist, but the first attempt failed and the fish took off again.

I thought my strength would give out completely. I almost didn't care. Let him take line if he could. This was the king of fish in his own environment. If he broke free now, could I really complain after such a magnificent fight? I had had the ultimate fishing experience and the outcome now was almost an irrelevancy. Almost, but not quite. This was my fish and I wanted him!

The salmon was back on a short line and there was Brian with the fish expertly gaffed in the Norwegian way and bringing him ashore. I had played the fish on a fly-rod through three beats, three sets of rapids and one and a half miles of river. The fish was shining silver, and covered with sea-lice. He was four feet long and had a thirty-inch girth. The verified time of the encounter was one hour fifteen minutes, and when put on the scales the fish weighed forty-nine and a half pounds.

PROVOST JOHN BURNESS'S 50lb BERVIE BAY SALMON
No. 3

Dr Derek Mills, one of Britain's best-known fishery biologists, has helped me on a number of occasions. Recently, he sent a newspaper cutting depicting an angler holding the dorsal fin of a 50lb cock salmon with one hand and what appears to be a 15ft salmon fly rod with the other. In the caption the angler is named as Provost John Burness and the location of the catch is given as Bervie Bay. Now Bervie Bay is a saltwater bay, some 12 miles north of Montrose in Aberdeenshire. But I am afraid this information presents us with a problem, because the inference is that we are looking at the first salmon over 50lb ever to be caught on a fly in saltwater. I think it unlikely, but what are we to make of these data?

The Bervie Water runs into Bervie Bay at Inverbervie but it is hard to believe that

Provost John Burness with the 50lb salmon he landed in Bervie Bay.

Bervie Bay

such a small river was the intended destination of this huge fish. More likely it was destined to run up the North Esk, a river just 9 miles farther south that is known for big fish, having produced salmon of 50lb in 1889, 63lb in 1890, 53lb in 1901 and 55lb in 1925.

There is a possibility that the fish was taking a look at, or rather a sniff of, the Bervie Water and found itself in the sea pool of that river, which would have a high freshwater content after heavy rainfall. Sea pools, particularly on smaller rivers, are sometimes quite productive for rod fishermen.

A good example of a productive sea pool is to be found on the Screebe River in County Mayo. The following report, under the headline 'Shark on a Salmon Line', appeared in the *Daily Mail* on 17 July 1905:

> Mr. Howard St. George, writing from Maam Cross, Connemara, to the *Irish Times*, tells a remarkable story of the catching of a shark, which is now on view in Dublin. While fishing at the mouth of the Screebe River, Mr. Hugh Gore, a friend of Mr. St. George, was playing a salmon when it was seized by some large fish. A struggle with the latter ensued lasting an hour and a half, during which half a mile was covered. Finally the strange fish was brought to the beach and landed. It proved to be a shark nearly 5 ft. in length and 2 ft. in girth.

Incidentally, Howard St George was a very well-known salmon angler who killed a 51lb salmon on a Jock Scott fly on the Tweed in 1921 (see *Giant Salmon*, Vol. 1, p.91).

Using his contact skills, my friend David Hatwell got in touch with the Inverbervie Library and what follows is an extract from his letter to me, followed by a newspaper report published in 1966.

I contacted Joan Anderson at Inverbervie Library, who put me on to historian

Mr Beattie. His father took over as Provost from John Burness and recalls that the fish caused quite a stir at the time. It was exhibited in the Crown Hotel.

I then received an email from Mr Beattie's niece, Mrs Margaret Gray, enclosing the press report and a copy of the original photo.

Excitement at Inverbervie

Salmon and seatrout leaping the falls of a Highland river make a great spectacle. And also when they leap in salt water, as they often do in the bay at Inverbervie. The gravelly bay is a gathering ground for finnock, seatrout, grilse and salmon, and often they start leaping about quite close inshore. Sometimes they are caught on rod and line, but it's not easy 'running' a salmon which has the whole of the North Sea to turn to!

The first notable salmon caught on the beach here was taken 30 years ago by Inverbervie's Provost Burness.

The Provost armed himself with a 17-foot rod, 200 yards of the best Bervie-made flax line, and a steel trace.

The Battle

All afternoon he cast into the heavy seas. Then, near dusk, he hooked a powerful fish, which had him plunging back and forth along the foreshore. He could make little of it, and it began to get really dark. At last, sodden and exhausted, the Provost announced to his two companions that he was going to try and beach his capture.

'Wait, wait!' he was advised. 'It's noo played oot yet!'

'Weel, if it's noo, I AM!' said the Provost, and brought in the salmon on a breaking wave.

It was gaffed by torchlight in the streaming water and gravel as the wave fell back, and dragged up the beach in triumph. Then they carried it up the steep path to the square, and had a look at it in the light of a street lamp.

What a fish it was! No less than 4ft. 4in. long and touching 50lb.

The above is an excellent report that gives us some precise details – length of rod (17 feet), length of line (200 yards), tied to a steel trace. Curiously, it follows that Burness must have been fly fishing at the time, simply because you cannot cast a bait out with a 17-foot fly rod and a Nottingham-type reel.

The report settles the weight argument emphatically by using the phrase 'touching 50lb' (one newspaper reported a weight of 52lb) and gives a length of 52in. There is a date on the cutting indicating that the fish was caught in 1937.

STIAN HAMMERSVIK'S 50lb ALTEN RIVER SALMON
No. 4

On 2 August 2007, a male salmon weighing half an ounce over 50lb was caught on a fly called the African Beauty in the Bollo Pool on the Alten River. This was the heaviest of three big fish caught by the same angler that day.

My friend David Hatwell was given these details by Stian Hammersvik on a video. It would seem from the returns that Norwegian rivers, and in particular the Alten, were even better in 2008, producing well above average catches of 50lb-plus salmon.

Stian described the fly that lured the above fine fish thus: 'The fly was big, black and fluffy. It had a red butt and silver rib. There was some Jungle cock on the side'.

DR DRUMMOND'S 50lb 8oz GRAND CASCAPEDIA SALMON
No. 5

According to angling correspondent C.B.B., writing in *Outing Magazine* in December 1890, when the opportunity arose, it was a fairly common practice during the later nineteenth century for anglers in Maine, Michigan, Wisconsin and northern Canada to kill such numbers of trout and bass as would enable them to take 'show-off' photographs of a 'one-day catch' before it was 'thrown aside in the bushes'. But, apparently, this was not the case with salmon, since by then salmon fishermen had become fully aware of the scarcity of their quarry and its need of their protection.

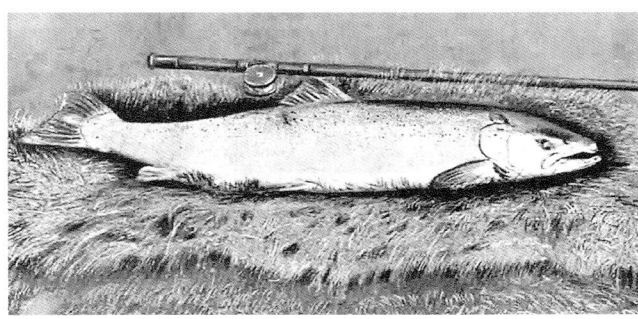

It is surprising that Dr Drummond's fish is illustrated with a drawing, albeit a fine one, since we know from C.B.B.'s account that by the 1890s cameras were in vogue and carried by anglers.

C.B.B. then proceeded with this catch report:

> Among the successful salmon catches of the present year is that of Dr W.H. Drummond, of Montreal, who scored a 'river king', the true salmon, Salmo salar, weighing fifty pounds and eight ounces, the largest recorded salmon caught this year on any of the Canadian rivers, and the next largest fish of the species that has ever been landed by rod and reel in America, the record being held by J.W. Dunn, who, a few years ago, killed on the same river a fifty-four pound fish.
>
> Dr Drummond's specimen was taken on Wednesday, June 25, on the Grand Cascapedia, with a very large Lansdowne fly.

Hoagy B. Carmichael wrote a lovely cameo on Dr William Henry Drummond in his excellent profile, *The Grand Cascapedia River: A History* (2006). He tells us that Drummond caught his fish from a boat on a big single-iron Lansdowne Dee fly in a driving rainstorm. Drummond migrated to Canada from Ireland in 1856 and became a famous 'dialect' poet, who devoted much of his time trying to draw English-speaking and French-speaking people together.

HEIKE KEMPPAINEN'S
50lb 12oz ORKLA RIVER SALMON
—— No. 8 ——

The late-season (August 2008), copper-coloured male salmon shown in these photographs is probably the largest fly-caught fish ever taken from Norway's Orkla River. Kemppainen was using one of his own home-tied flies. The salmon was 52in long.

This salmon's gape shows how easy it must be for such a large fish to swallow a herring – with alacrity and consummate efficiency.

SHIRLEY DETERDING'S 51lb ALTEN RIVER SALMON
No. 9

Shirley Deterding's skills as one of Britain's outstanding women salmon fishers were proved when, in August 2006, she caught a 51lb salmon on Norway's famed Alten River, taking it from Langstilla Pool on the Stengelsen beat.

Shirley Deterding, rather refreshingly, sent me a note that, instead of being the usual catch account, gives readers an insight into the experience of fishing what is unquestionably the world's most productive, and exclusive, river for fly-caught Atlantic salmon weighing over 50lb. (In July 2008, three salmon of over 50lb were caught in ten days.)

Shirley Deterding with her boatman, Paul Kristian Olausen, and her big fish.

This photograph of the Alten River shows what fly fishing for salmon must be like on a river geographically placed within the Arctic Circle.

In August 2006 I was fortunate enough to be invited to fish the Alta River in Norway. This was serious Atlantic salmon fishing on one of the world's most beautiful and unspoiled rivers with some of the most experienced fishermen in the world.

The Alta River is divided into three sections, as it is a long river of some 40 miles, the lower beat being the base camp and nearest to the sea, the middle beat privately owned, and the top beat over the waterfall at the top of the river.

During the week each fisherman spends one or two nights at the mid-camp and top camp, each part being very different landscape and fishing: some narrow canyons, some very rapid rocky and dangerous parts, and some wide flat pools which hold a lot of fish in the dark depths. Each camp has an excellent chef and staff and although there is no electricity they prepare and serve the most fantastic meals on an old wood stove. Lunchtime on the river bank around a camp fire is all part of the excitement and beauty of this wonderful northern wilderness river.

To get to the top beat requires carrying all the luggage and overnight equipment over a steep and difficult climb above the falls, where other boats are ready to take you on up river to fish and to the top cabin. Each boat has a guide and an experienced boatman and one fisherman! Most of the portage falls on the guide and boatman and it is an arduous climb! They are wonderful and kind people and help make the week an experience of a lifetime. The people working in the lodges are there for the period of time of the fishing and all food and equipment has to be carried up in the motorized canoes and over the falls, a tough trip!

It is not possible to fish the River Alta unless you are a member or guest of the very exclusive syndicate, or a resident of the small town of Alta where the fishing is free but restricted to various times. All fish are returned to the river now, although this was not always the case.

The week went quickly by with a lot of hard work, many casts and taking one's turn on the less popular beats. The scenery was awe-inspiring. By the end of the week I had caught 26 fish [including] 11 grilse and two gigantic salmon over 40lb, my biggest being 51lb.

All fish were caught on the same fly, a Norwegian green and yellow tube fly called an Olive Phantom, except a 33lb fish, which was caught on a Red Francis. I used an intermediate line, Sage rod and a Bogdan reel borrowed from my guide. One fish was caught on a sinking line and three on a floating line with a sink tip.

SIR DAVID HOARE'S 51lb ALTEN RIVER SALMON
No. 10

In January 2008 it came to my notice that Sir David Hoare had recently caught a big Alten salmon on fly. Sir David kindly gave me a copy of the catch account, culled from a letter he had written to his American friend Nat Reed (who keeps a fishing diary) soon after his arrival at Sandia Lodge in early July 2007. This entry first appeared in the reprint of the first volume of *Giant Salmon*.

Our arrival at Sandia Lodge was as welcoming as ever and we enjoyed an excellent dinner there. Afterwards we set off down river and through the rapids to Gilvo. The water level had dropped to around 1ft 7in and the dark strong current of that great pool looked so enticing. However, we saw no sign of a fish so dropped down carefully to negotiate the wild and rugged Battagoski rapids, which lead one into Snoski. The river valley here is very narrow and wild with steep rocks on either side. It is a pool I love to fish as the current is smooth and powerful and works the fly to perfection. However, within my memory, over eighteen years no fish has even shown there, let alone risen to a fly. Fishing from the left bank with my old original 15ft Sage rod and Orvis intermediate line, and Grand Cascapedia reel and

Sir David (left) and his boatman, Olaf Haldorsen. Notice the pinkish sheen of the fish's back – that unfailing indication of a fresh-run fish.

Seagur nylon cast, I worked my way carefully down to a rock where the current gathers pace and always seems a likely holding lie. Something rose at my Brooks, and rings spread out across the surface. I tried two more casts but to no avail so decided to pick up my other rod, a 15ft Thomas & Thomas with a sinking line and an ally shrimp tube. This would get down to the fish and maybe arouse more interest and I was sure of receiving a long steady pull and draw. However, to my dismay, it was met with utter disdain, so we drew back to consider what other tactics to adopt.

On arrival at Stengelsen I had picked up some specially tied Green Highlanders from the local fly tier and so chose a delicate size six treble, lightly dressed, and changed the Brooks for this. Right beside the stone again, on the edge of the current, there was a gentle rise and the line tightened. I slowly lifted the rod and met a resistance that felt like the rock itself. Within seconds the fish took off downstream in a really powerful run and we leapt into the boat. However, within a short space of time the salmon had turned and was heading back up the other side of the river towards the rapids. How far that fish ascended those rapids I do not know but 250 yards of line and backing had left my reel. Fortunately, there was still some to spare. I applied strong pressure and eventually the fish turned, descended the rapids and re-entered the pool, and fought very deep for the next hour. We took the boat down to calmer waters alongside the cliff and once the salmon almost broached the surface; it made two very determined runs towards the opposite bank, some 40 yards away. Yan, my boatman and netter, stayed very calm as always and held the net very deep and still in the water as I trusted my hook hold and pulled the fish to the surface. For the first time, as the net closed in on our quarry, we were able to gauge the size and shape of this salmon. It was a perfect specimen, fresh from the ocean, very deep and in perfect proportion to its length, a male with little lower jaw developed as yet. We fetched the new scales from the boat and the balance showed 23.2 kilos (exactly 51lb). The fish measured 50in length and 32in girth.

That was exciting enough but what was to follow doubled my elation. We quickly slipped the fly out with no difficulty, took various photographs and measurements and placed the fish back in the river in a channel close to the bank. He sat on his pectoral fins and belly for a full ten minutes, bubbles of air rising from his gills and other vents. Then, ever so slowly he swam away upstream and we bade farewell and took to the whisky bottle as my legs turned to jelly. However, several minutes later he reappeared and swam very slowly past us again with a knowing look in his eye. For the next half hour he swam large circles and made no effort to enter the hard current of the river. Eventually, we decided he should be encouraged to enter into deeper water again, so I climbed down the bank and into the sandy bed of the channel and he swam alongside my legs like a tame dolphin. I walked out as far as I dared and he followed me until he caught the hard current and drifted off, hopefully on his way back to the spawning beds.

He was a noble fish who seemed to show gratitude at being released. Seven years ago to the same night, I caught and killed a fish of 49lb after two hours and a hard fight in high water. because we wanted to make sure we had landed a 50-pounder and the scales to prove it were back in camp. How wrong we were on both counts and I regret to this day having killed that fish.

The behaviour of this salmon was extraordinary but I shall resist the temptation to attempt to provide an explanation. This much is certain, though – it owed its life to the unnecessary death of the 49-pounder. That event had disciplined the unwitting sportsman to carry weighing scales with him whenever he fishes the world's most abundant producer of rod-caught 50-pounders taken with the fly – Norway's River Alten.

DAVID CLARKE'S 51lb ALTEN RIVER SALMON
No. 11

Although 2009 was a disappointing year for giant salmon on the Alten – given that it is the world's premier salmon river for fly-caught 50-pounders – there were a few successes. On 13 July, David Clarke caught his 51lb fish on a Temple Dog fly from Richard Holla Pool (or Richard's Hole). I am grateful to the Alta Association for providing this information via the internet.

There was good reason for all members of this team to smile – namely Scotsman David Clarke and his two boatmen, Sverre Jørgen (left) and Jørgen Emaus. Look at the depth of the tail fin when compared with the boatman's hand.

JAMES GREENWOOD'S 51½lb ALTEN RIVER SALMON
No. 14

On 5 July 2008, James Greenwood of Horsham in Sussex caught a fine 51½lb cock salmon on Norway's famous Alten River, and in January 2009 he sent me two superb photographs of his fish, one of which is reproduced below.

After some correspondence, James agreed to write a short account of his adventure, which I received on 7 July 2009.

James Greenwood's 51½lb fish

I was the guest of my cousin Rupert Lea (a regular Alta rod) and was fishing Ted Dalenson's rod (as he was away for three nights). I was using my own reel and line but Ted's rod.

The second night we were on one of the lower beats, and Rupert connected with several fish while I drew a blank in the first few hours of fishing. Then we arrived at Langstilla pool. The boat was hugging the bank and made casting very difficult. The first three attempts resulted in two bushes and one line-wrapped oar! I finally managed a fairly respectable cast and as it fished round we had a strong take in the middle of the fast water. The fish immediately took off directly across the river and took out at least 150m of line, and the run ended with the fish doing a most spectacular cartwheel. When this happened, the whole boat went quiet! I was blissfully unaware at that moment as to the size of the fish. I knew it was fairly big, but the head boatman said, 'It's big,' followed by our oarsman saying, 'It's very big.' Let battle commence. I kept as much pressure on as I dared (I had put on new 30lb frog nylon, and a new hook to go with the Baldrick tube) and the two boatmen manoeuvred us into the main part of the river. All the time we were slowly drifting downstream, with the fish making several good runs, each of which took me to my backing – a vast amount of reeling in line as fast as I could; arms beginning to ache as the battle continued and the half hour came and went; then a brief rest at the tip of a set of rapids. Do we try to stop it from going farther downstream or do we run the rapids and hope it stays on? We decided to go down the rapids, as there was a vast shingle bank that would afford us the ideal place to net it. All went to plan and forty-nine minutes later and 1½ miles downstream, he was in the net (after three rather heart-stopping attempts!). He sat very quietly in the net while we weighed him and after the photos had been taken he recovered rapidly and swam off strongly. The time was 23.45 by the time we landed him.

Summarizing the rest of James's letter, it would appear that his three-day spell on the Alten produced nine fish averaging 34½lb apiece. Most of them were caught on the Baldrick tube fly, although a 40¾lb fish was taken on a Temple Dog. Obviously, these two fly patterns are the ones to have about you, if you are ever lucky enough to be invited to fish on the Alten.

THORIEIF HAMMARI'S
51¾lb ALTEN RIVER SALMON
No. 15

Thorieif Hammari caught his 51lb 12oz salmon in the Alten River in 2007. Although I have not as yet received a capture account of this beautifully conditioned fish, I do know the name of the photographer – Runi Østiyngen, whose photograph was featured on a Norwegian website for sportsfishermen (www.fishing-norway.com).

Hammari's fish has the bodyline of a hen fish that could well have been covered in sea lice when it was caught.

MORTON SEAMAN'S 52lb ALTEN RIVER SALMON
No. 17

Green Highlander

'For most fishermen, the landing of a 50lb plus salmon is the fulfilment of a lifetime's dream. Landing two fish of that calibre must be an intoxicating experience. Morton Seaman, from the USA, took a fish weighing 51lb from Nedre Sierra pool on a Green Highlander fly, on 11 July 1992. His second big fish, weighing 52lb, fell to a Black and Silver tube fly at Langstilla on 9 July 1994. This information comes from the Alten Records.' This entry first appeared in the reprint of the first volume of *Giant Salmon*.

The above paragraph represented my limited knowledge of Morton Seaman's fish when *Giant Salmon* went to press in October 2007. Shortly afterwards, Nick Lyons wrote to me, advising me that he felt sure his friend Morton Seaman would provide a photograph of the larger fish, together with an account of its capture, if I contacted him, using the address supplied.

In the event, following my request, I received one of the finest photographs of a fresh-run salmon that I have ever seen – together with a catch account, laced with relaxed humour of a kind that is only likely to be forthcoming from one who had already (two years previously) caught a 'fish of a lifetime'.

After three days of slow angling, we started back to the lodge at 4.00 a.m. and stopped at the great Langstilla Pool for just one more try, because since childhood I have been addicted with the compulsion for one last try.

I cast my tube fly into the fast water along the far bank and the

In the annals of big-fish photography, this picture of Morton Seaman holding his 52-pounder must rank as one of the greatest ever. It is light years ahead of fish photographed in front of a bed sheet hanging on a washing line, or any other artificially created background.

salmon boiled but did not take. I cast again, stripped back at a medium rate, and the fish failed again. This merely caused me a small coronary.

Our boatman said I was stripping too fast. I disagreed, but it is a mistake to argue with a boatman after four years of employing his services and realizing he has been right 99 percent of the time. I made several more casts and retrieved with very, very slow strips. The fly was in slow water, four or five feet deep, when the fish took and raced powerfully for the center of the pool. Then he jumped as we paddled towards shore, and in the half light looked fairly large. Suddenly, the fish launched into a hundred-yard run down river! I couldn't slow him or budge him. I told the boatman that the fish now felt really big, to which he replied, 'That's what you always say.' I'd thought we'd have to follow the fish down but it soon returned to the main pool – and then it took a full hour, gaining and losing line, and then gaining it again, to bring him close.

The last fifteen minutes were scary. The salmon splashed his huge tail and kept reminding me that I had on a sixteen-pound-test tippet. We didn't gaff the fish but sort of shoved him up on the bank, and the boatman and his helper both quickly fell on the beauty – the great fish shaped like a grilse and covered with sea lice. He was a catch of my life number two. Then someone brought out vodka and soon we were all laughing and talking at once and both men kept shaking my quivering hand.

This, I believe, is the elaborate story of my fish. I hope you find it interesting.

MAJOR CUNARD'S 52lb RIVER TAY SALMON
No. 18

Sometimes the most unlikely circumstances lead to the discovery of a new entry for this book. Major Cunard's whopping great Tay salmon, which he caught on a fly in 1907, is a case in point.

In October 2009 my wife and I found ourselves comfortably based in a gem of a sixteenth-century eating house, Ye Olde Beehive Inne in Newholm, some two miles north of Whitby. From local gossip my radar soon picked up the tale of a big salmon that was fixed to the wall of another inn – the Wheatsheaf in Egton, some 6 miles farther north. It turned out that the Wheatsheaf, with a reputation for cuisine that matched the Beehive's, housed a collection of angling memorabilia owned by its proprietor Nigel Pulling.

For an hour and a half I put question after question to poor Mr Pulling, at a time when he was frenetically busy, and managed to glean some valuable information. Curiously, although we have come to expect catch data to be displayed on a plaque located somewhere on the front of the case, or painted by hand on the bow-fronted glass in black-edged gold letters, it was not so with this Malloch-mounted fish. The legend was written on the back of the case.

Mr Pulling remembered a few of the more important back-of-the-case details – the fish was caught by Major Cunard on a fly, it had taken 4 hours and 20 minutes to subdue and it was a cock fish. We measured it at 46½in from its nose to the fork of its tail, and 48in to the tip of its tail. The measurement to the tip is the more likely to have been recorded at the time of capture.

Major Cunard's salmon – on view at the Wheatsheaf Inn at Egton, Yorkshire.

JOHN MACMILLAN'S
52lb ALTEN RIVER SALMON
No. 19

Ivar Leinan kindly identified the three people depicted, together with an exceedingly large salmon:

> The 52-pounder was caught by John MacMillan in Sautso, Kotaniemi (in front of the lodge), August 23, 2003. His boatmen are Sverre J. Romsdal (left) and Magnus Paulsen (right).

I am always more impressed with a photograph of a large salmon when I notice a human hand – in this case, Sverre J. Romsdal's right hand – close to the fish's adipose fin. Some fin – some fish!

CHARLES BALBACH'S
52½lb ALTEN RIVER SALMON
No. 20

When Mollie Fitzgerald of Frontiers, the travel consultants, alerted me to the taking of this fish, I wrote to Charles Balbach at his New York home and received the following reply:

I am pleased and proud to share with you the details of catching my large salmon. The cock fish weighed 52½lb. It was 50 inches long and had a 27 inch girth with an 11 inch wide tail. I caught the fish on 23rd June 2008 at 8.45 p.m. in the Bollo Pool on the Alta River. I was using a tube fly with a #6 treble hook. I had risen the fish earlier, on another fly, but it didn't come back, so we moved up to the head of the pool and changed to a Pahtakorva fly that my guide, Tormod Mosesen, took from his box.

I have included an account of the capture of the fish (which took about forty minutes) written by my boat companion and good friend Peter Dominick, who is an architect in Denver, Colorado.

Thank you for allowing me to share the story of a great night of good luck on the Alta River.

Day one, 23 June: on the first pool the river was 4ft over its mark and rising (during the week it went to 6½ft over, making it by degrees unrecognisable).

It was raining hard and quite cold. We were fishing with Tormod Mosesen, the famous guide whom we read about in your *Domesday Book of Giant Salmon* – the same boatman who had helped Clare de Burgh land a 53-pounder in 1968 after an epic 2½ hour battle.

We entered at the top of the pool at approximately 8.30 p.m. The fish rose almost on the first cast but did not take – we changed flies, Charles cast again and it took. Almost instantaneously, the reel fell off the rod into the bottom of the boat and the fish, with no pressure on it, swam aimlessly around in deep quiet water while Tormod tried to get the reel back on the rod. The screw seats were jammed and he could get no purchase. The fish began to move and while Charles held the rod, I held the reel to the butt as he began the fight. It was a bit awkward to say the least. A couple of times it slipped loose and Tormod was yelling to watch out and keep the line taut.

Tormod Mosesen with his son Karstein, who is holding the 52½lb salmon.

This was Tormod's 48th year on the Alta as a guide and Charles's 19th year as a fisherman. I was the rookie along with Tormod's son, Karstein, trying to sort out what was the best way to handle the problem. Suddenly, the fish spun out into the current and the line began to tear away into the backing. Charles, with four hands, was having a fine time, just letting it run until Tormod suggested that we all had to move. So the boat pulled out into the current as well, and slid down river with the fish for several hundred yards . . . slowly, Charles worked him back to the quiet water. We seemed to have been at a standstill for some time when Tormod had us get out of the boat and back on to the shore. I had my arms around Charles, walking behind him, holding the reel to the rod. We had not seen the fish but there was a sense that it was a big one from the way it behaved – strong, surly, a head shaker, like a huge brown [trout] . . . Charles worked it smoothly but determinedly, if somewhat uncomfortably with me holding him in a bear hug from behind.

Closer and closer till Karstein had the net ready, it swirled away several times, finally showing the size of its tail. Tormod began to yell excitedly, 'It's a monster, it's huge, it's over 25 kilo. God, what a fish!'

Then, suddenly, it was in the net – maybe thirty minutes, maybe less. We weighed it in the net. Tormod declared we must take it, so it was killed and weighed again. Then Jim Schneider showed up and we weighed it again with his boat's net – both confirmed 52½lb. It measured 50 inches by 27 inches with an 11-inch spread to its tail. Another Alta special! What a beauty!

In such a situation, cool heads are required and split-second responses. During the battle, the four people involved all assumed their vital roles, but it is remarkable that in the end they succeeded. They should have lost this fish, because the tackle was not properly checked.

RUPERT LEA'S
52lb 10oz ALTEN RIVER SALMON
No. 21

Through the good offices of his cousin James Greenwood (who also caught a 50-pounder), I was able to obtain two photographs of Rupert Lea's shapely hen salmon. He caught it in Snoski Pool, on Norway's Alten River, on 9 July 2008. This is his catch account.

The start of the salmon fishing season of 2008 was notable for the very high water level – at 5 foot above normal summer level, usually 2–3 feet – combined with what appeared to be a good run of salmon, including some heavy fish.

Dropping down some rapids, we started to fish a pool called Snoski. Although a dark, deep pool, I felt some excitement as Snoski occasionally yields a few large salmon. We approached the big fish 'taking spot', a small patch of water around a triangular rock protruding out the water on the inside of the main stream. Despite great anticipation – nothing happened. A few minutes later our boat was tucked in behind that rock, leaving my fly to hang over the best taking place, while I continued, rather despairingly, to cast, or due to lack of enthusiasm, 'chuck' my line out. Suddenly, somewhere in the deep swirls, my line stopped moving towards the boat and began to leave my reel at high speed. The fish moved upstream steadily, jumping twice, revealing that it was a large fish. Upon reaching the rapids upstream, the fish had a 'sulky' period before deciding to head back downstream through the canyon. After 55 minutes, the fish was eventually netted and unhooked with some difficulty, due to the very steep river banks.

The two boatmen (seen in the photograph) and I were surprised that I had caught a hen fish. The weight, 23.85 kilos (52.58lb), was a bit disappointing given its length at 54in. Surprisingly for this river, the fish would seem to have been present for at least a month. Female salmon on the Alta make their first spawning run as two sea-winter fish, with an average weight of 24lb, second-time spawners typically weigh 35lb. It would appear that our fish was a fourth- or fifth-time spawner. Something of a miracle in itself. She was hooked at 11.45 p.m. on July 8 and landed at 12.40 (00.40) a.m. on July 9. The fly was a 3-inch Temple Dog. After lunch (at 1 a.m.), we had three more salmon, 24, 26 and 34lb. On returning to the lodge, a few whiskies were poured and drunk by fishers and boatmen. During the conversation that followed I was sharply corrected by one of our boatmen when I made the observation that it was remarkable to catch a 50lb fish that was a 'girl'. The response was immediate – 'More like a grandmother.' My many thanks to Trond and Foro, my boatmen on that night.

Rupert Lea's fish being held by the boatmen, Trond and Foro.

Rupert Lea playing his fish.

A 52lb 10oz MORRUM RIVER SALMON
No. 22

Sweden's Morrum River is famous for its unparalleled rod-caught, double-figure sea trout. Furthermore, since the late 1970s it has produced from its thirty keepered beats at least ten salmon weighing 50lb or more – all caught on fly.

This photograph appeared in Bob Church's This Fishing Life. *Sadly, Bob is unable to identify the captor of this magnificent salmon.*

TOR JOHNNY SIVERTSEN'S 52lb 11½oz REPPARFJORD RIVER SALMON
No. 23

On 10 July 2009 Tor Johnny Sivertsen caught his magnificent salmon on a Cascade shrimp tube-fly in Josefsen Pool. It is a record for a river that is not well known to British anglers. Repparfjord River stretches for more than 46 miles (75km) – long by Norwegian standards – and is famous for its scenic beauty, particularly where it flows through the Sennalandet highlands. Lake Storvatnet, in the same catchment area, is well known for its runs of migratory charr.

This photograph of Tor Johnny Sivertsen and his salmon is unusual in showing the fish half-in and half-out of water.

A 53lb VEFSEN RIVER SALMON
No. 24

Early last century, Captain C.E. Radclyffe contributed to a publication entitled *Fishing*, published by *Country Life* (London, 1904). In a section devoted to the Vefsen River, Radclyffe describes the three foremost beats:

> For many years the three best beats on the river have been held by three sportsmen, who are fortunate to have secured long leases of the water. The lowest beat, called Stjernberg, is held by Mr. R. Venables Kyrke. Above this comes a beat of some three miles in extent, which includes the celebrated Foss Pool below Forsjord Foss. This beat is held by Major Chadwick, and is a particularly fine stretch of harling water. Above Forsjord Foss comes another fine stretch of water, extending some eight or ten miles to another big foss, called Laksfoss. This beat is held by Mr. Kyrke and Colonel W.E. Brymer. To Mr. Kyrke a considerable amount of credit is due for the improvement of the Vefsen. At no inconsiderable trouble and expense, he has erected a ladder at Forsjord Foss, up which salmon can ascend in high water.

If readers refer to page 267 of *Giant Salmon*, they will read about a number of huge salmon, including a 60-pounder, that were subsequently caught on Mr Kyrke's water. Prior to 1903, however, the largest rod-caught salmon came from Major Chadwick's beat.

> Like all northern rivers, the run of fish is late on the Vefsen, and the river is at its best during July. Salmon run up to big weights, but, as the author has observed on other Norwegian rivers, the heaviest fish are generally taken on the lower reaches, the very heavy fish evidently not liking the knocking about which they receive in running over the fosses and salmon passes. Fish have been taken on Major Chadwick's beat up to 53lbs. weight, but above Forsjord Foss the heaviest fish on record appears to be 43lbs., although many have been taken there of 40lbs. and over.

It looks very much as though the 53lb fish was caught on a fly using the preferred method – harling. Radclyffe recommended the following patterns:

The best patterns for this river may be classed as follows, according to particulars supplied to the writer by one of the most experienced anglers on the river. The Durham Ranger is a great favourite, Silver Doctor and Dusty Miller are good for bright weather, and the Jock Scott is good at any time. The Black Dose and Black Doctor are excellent for night and evening fishing, and also the Alexandra.

WILLY THOMASSEN'S 53lb ALTEN RIVER SALMON
No. 25

In November 2008, I received notification of Willy Thomassen's salmon together with a photograph (albeit not a very good one). The fish was taken from Øvre-Sorrisniva Pool on the Alten River on 7 August 1995. From the nature of the regulations on the Alten River at that time of year, we can be pretty sure that the fish was caught on fly and that it was a cock fish, because of the kyped jaw.

From the part of the fish that is included in the photograph, it seems clear that the claimed weight is fully justified, but how sad it is that when you catch the fish of a lifetime, your photographer chops out half of it, and part of your legs!

THE LATCHFORD CAUSEY 54lb SALMON
No. 30

One of the earliest salmon weighing over 50lb of which I have knowledge is mentioned on page 169 of Richard Brookes' fourth edition of *The Art of Angling* (T. Lowndes, 1774) – and David Beazley, the librarian of the Flyfishers Club, assures me that the note is also in the earlier editions. In his short chapter on salmon, Richard Brookes writes, 'Their greatest magnitude is much the same in most parts of Europe, and when they are largest, they weigh from 36 to 54 pounds; one of this last weight being caught at Latchford Causey, in Year 1763.'

When I tried to locate Latchford Causey on a map of Britain, I drew a blank, coming up with just two places named Latchford. One was close to the River Mersey in Cheshire and the other near the River Rib in Hertfordshire. I dismissed the latter because I could not conceive of a 54lb salmon in such a small chalk stream.

Having settled on the Mersey alternative, in March 2008 I contacted my friend Dr Malcolm Greenhalgh, who lives nearby in Warrington. Malcolm told me that the Causey part of the place name was dropped when the builders of the Manchester ship canal incorporated a long section of the river during the canal's construction. There was more. Apparently, there had long been a salmon netting station at Latchford Causey, which had survived until industrial pollution reduced the salmon runs to an unsustainable economic level.

In the 1940 October/December issue of the magazine *Angling*, Eric Hardy F.Z.S. wrote a piece about the salmon rivers in the north west of England. While he was explaining the sewage problem on the river Dee, he mentioned the Mersey:

> Domestic sewage and manurial effluents were the chief pollution, but the damage was not nearly so great as that on the Mersey, where salmon were exterminated by the twentieth century.

Sad to say, Mersey salmon had disappeared, that is until 2001, when a salmon (and three sea trout) were netted at the weir at Warrington. Amazingly, when an experimental trap was used at the weir in 2006, forty-one salmon were trapped in eight days. Doubtless these fish were heading for the upper reaches (above Stockport) where salmon smolts have been recorded. Seemingly, the present salmon stock is growing because of a cleaner river, despite the fact that no re-stocking has been attempted. The runs have happened because stray salmon from other rivers are now in the process of repopulating the Mersey system. In time, perhaps the Mersey could reclaim its position in the premier league of English salmon rivers, as it was in 1806, when Alexander Mackintosh, on page 7 of his famous book *The Driffield Angler*, included the River Mersey in his list of the thirteen chief rivers in England that yield this excellent fish.

This fine late eighteenth century engraving of the River Mersey at Latchford (now in the Warrington archive) shows three fishermen – two on the shore and one in a boat – working with a seine net. Three more fishermen wait for the boatman to complete his manoeuvre and bring his end of the rope to the bank so that the six men (three on each rope) could draw the net ashore. Closer inspection reveals an angler, fishing from the high ground just in front of the three trees. It is worth noting what Alan Crosby recorded in A History of Warrington (Phillimore, 2002) when he quoted details of a letter written in 1698 by Thomas Patten to Richard Norris about over-fishing of the River Mersey: 'Vast numbers of salmon trout are taken, so as to supply all the Country, and Market Towns 20 miles round, and when the Country is cloyed [full up] or when they cannot get sale for them, they give them to their swine . . .'

EINAR ANTONSEN'S 54lb ALTEN RIVER SALMON
No. 32

In November 2008, I received a note from David Hatwell advising me that a 54lb salmon had been taken from the Alten River at Midterfaret on 1 July 2000 – a millennium fish no less. The July date is pretty good evidence that the fish was caught on a fly, but as yet I have not managed to find a full catch account.

Various faults are revealed in this photograph. Firstly, the fishermen have been forced to close their eyes because they are staring directly at the sun. Secondly, since two people have chosen to stand close together with the catch, the camera should have been turned 90° so as to produce an upright configuration. Thirdly, the cameraman was positioned too close to the men and the fish, so their heads and feet and the fish's jaw have been clipped off. It should be recorded, however, that worse things sometimes happen in photography.

MOLLIE FITZGERALD'S 54lb ALTEN RIVER SALMON
— No. 33 —

Mollie Fitzgerald, one of the co-owners of Frontiers, a company that specializes in arranging game-fishing trips to almost every continent, caught a 54-pounder on Norway's Alten River on 28 June 2008.

When I contacted Mollie, she very kindly sent me the following catch account:

We set out on night number four of our usual fishing week, 24–30 June, with not a lot of optimism. The river was the highest I'd ever seen it in my tenure on the river at 6½ feet. Many trees and bushes on the river's edge were submerged in water and it left very few fishable pools. In June, we fish from 8.00 p.m. to 4.00 a.m. with a coffee break around midnight. I had a nice fish at Upper Sierra before coffee, caught on a medium-fast sink line.

Mollie introduces a novel way of holding a big fish, cradling it on her knees – and she manages to convey to any onlooker how pleased she is with her catch.

We decided to rest the pool and went on to Vinagorva, the next pool up, to have a try there and were delighted with another fish, which was netted on the drift because we had no place to land it! We then decided to return to Upper Sierra – it was about 3.00 a.m. by this time, for another go with a sinktip. It's one of my favourite places on the river, where it makes a giant horseshoe turn. There's a lovely little cabin perched on the bank and it's a most attractive setting.

The fish took on the dangle, as they often do in high water and just as the fish earlier in the evening had done. The take was underwater and we did not see the fish until much later, but it pulled strong and hard and made a huge initial first run that caused much calamity in the boat! It fought for approximately 45 minutes with four big jumps, and we went downriver to Lower Sierra (through a set of rapids) and finally landed the fish at the lunch spot at Lower Sierra. The gravel bar/beach area that is normally there was completely submerged and we were very worried about losing the fish because of the number of sapling trees underwater in which the fish could have gotten tangled, but my wonderful boatmen, Trond and Frode Simensen, prevailed. They were calm and collected throughout the battle, even as my anxiety mounted, and the effort was rewarded with a beautiful 24.5-kilo male fish (54lb). The fish measured 46 inches long by 28 inches girth, and was photographed and released in excellent condition.

Mikkeli Blue

This, as you know, is a short length measurement for a 50lb fish and, because of this, we did test the scales against two other sets of scales and I'm therefore confident that they [the measurements] were accurate. It's worth noting that this was an unusually shaped fish, quite fat from the head all the way through to its tail, and rather atypical of the normal Alta fish, which can be quite football shaped (American football!). In other words, it was fat in the middle but then tapering at the head and tail sections. It was caught on a 14 foot, 9 weight, Thomas & Thomas rod (my favourite), outfitted with a borrowed Sage reel with a Rio Windcutter Spey line 9/10/11.

The fly is a well-known Alta fly called Mikkeli Blue. It is a silver-bodied fly and this was a small one (about 1½ inches long) with a bit of blue and red accent colors. This fish trumped my previous best fish by 16lb.

THE ENGLISH TENANT'S 55lb SALMON FROM THE MAALES RIVER SYSTEM
No. 36

My favourite angling writer, save Sir Herbert Maxwell, is John Waller Hills. His *A History of Fly Fishing for Trout* (Philip Allan, 1921) is a book that I read again and again. *A Summer on the Test* (Philip Allan, 1924) is his most popular work. Indeed, it has been described – by Callahan and Morgan in a reprint of *Hampton's Angling Bibliography* (Three Beards Press, 2008) – as 'one of the most important fishing books of all time'. *My Sporting Life* (Philip Allan, 1936), which was published when the author was nearly 70 years old, is not so well known but is a fluent and mature work that seriously deserves to be reprinted. Most importantly, it contains a great rarity – a full description of the art (at least, the boatman's art) of harling, which is both illuminating and definitive.

In 1893, when Hills was 26 years old, he joined three other young men to fish the Maales River and its two tributaries, the Bardo and Malang, principally for salmon. His delightful description of fishing the Bardo helps us to understand why Norway has been such an inescapable lure to small groups of British salmon anglers for over 150 years.

> Bardo and Malang are big, heavy rivers, and mostly we harled. Harling consists in starting at the top of a pool, letting out twenty yards or so of line, and then your boatman crossing and recrossing the water, so as to swing your fly or spoon in the most enticing way over the salmon. I do not recommend harling. But, if anyone thinks it is unskilful and easy, let him try working the boat, where the real skill comes in. He will find that he has a very great deal to learn. And so I found from watching the manoeuvres of our admirable fishermen. I learnt much of the way to make a salmon take. When our boatmen spotted a salmon, they would go on at him until he took. First they would handle the boat so as to bring the lure steadily across him. If that failed, they would work it over him either more slowly or more sharply. Or they would impart an across-and-downwards movement, so that your fly slipped right by his eye, or they would let it down six or eight yards below the fish, row hard upstream, and bring it quickly and smoothly past him. If all failed they would dangle it wavering just in front of his nose. In the end they succeeded more often than not. And very instructive it was.

But salmon did not show much in those rivers, and most of our fishing was quartering the water. However, even then one could see how much skill was needed to keep your fly or spoon always working in a tumultuous river, full of eddies and washes, as well as boulders and sunken trees. Oh, there is much skill in harling for the boatmen. And these men were magnificent gaffers. They used six- or seven-foot shafts, and I have seen my man lie flat in the boat, bury his whole shaft and his arm up to the shoulder in the water, and yank up a twenty pounder which was kicking about at the bottom. You had to gaff as early as you could, taking risks which you need not take in Scotland, for you never knew what trees the last flood had jammed in the fairway.

My best fish was caught on September 11th, harling the prawn. I had killed one of 21½lb. in the morning, and went out again on the Bardo in the afternoon. It was a pleasant autumn day, not too cold. We harled steadily; nothing happened, and I got bored. The hills were frozen, consequently the river was lower than it ever had been before, and I was constantly getting hung up. Finally, I was really fast, and the boatman rowed downstream to get me free. I gave a great heave – I was using a three-ply trace – felt something give way, when suddenly the whole bottom of the river seemed to come to the top and a colossal salmon leapt into the air. My boatman yelled 'Fyrti pund lax,' and off this monster started as though he meant to reach the fjord. Off we went after him, full tilt, down that racing stream, my boatman, a fine hefty man, making the boat fly. In spite of his pace, the fish gained, my reel emptying fast. Suddenly there was a terrific shock, I was shot off the seat into the bottom of the boat, and there we were, jammed hard on a shallow. But this was a trifle to my boatman. He sprang overboard, seized the boat with one hand on each side of the gunwale, literally lifted it off the bottom, carried it to deep water, gave it a mighty shove off, jumped in and continued the pursuit. I looked at my reel: there were only a few turns of line left. I could see the pillar. But that run settled my fish. He was not strong, and fought no more. Nor was he forty pounds. He weighed 32 lb exactly. He was the build of a forty pounder, short and very deep, but he had probably been up since May, and had lost weight. However, one does not catch a thirty-two pounder every day of the week.

Three days before, I had had a very different experience. It was cold, it was raw, the sky was grey, there were patches of snow on the banks, and nothing had been caught for five days. Gone were the blazing evenings or mornings when the only trouble was to protect ourselves from mosquitoes.

Readers will have a problem if they try to find the Bardo River on a modern map. In 1908 the spelling was changed to Bardu. It is classed as one of Norway's best trout and charr rivers. John Waller Hills reckoned that he caught several grayling that weighed over 4lb and, later in life, regretted that he never actually weighed the bigger ones.

I was muffled up to the ears. We had harled and harled, and I grew colder and colder. Suddenly I hooked a beauty, a good twenty-five pounds weight, fresh run, tinted with violet, straight from the sea, one of those clean hard fish which you often catch in the autumn. We had him nearly killed, and were dropping easily downstream stern first to a convenient sandbank where many a salmon had been gaffed. The fish was below on a short line, not really pulling, just lurching and swirling about, carried along by the rattling current, and I was laughing and shouting with insolent triumph to my boatman. 'Ha, ha,' I said, 'here is our reward for long labour.' Suddenly the fish gave a sharp jump, my line was all too short, I did not drop my point, and my twisted trace snapped like cotton. My boatman rowed to shore, put his head between his hands, groaned and went on groaning. He waved aside my flask. We looked at each other with miserable eyes. And then, to make it worse, a fish, our fish, began splashing in the shallows across the river. He was getting rid of my prawn, dashing about, beating the water close to the surface, often throwing himself several feet in to the air. Upon my word, had I had my gun – I often carried one, as the duck were coming in on their flight south – I believe I could have shot him. But, after a bit, all was quiet: no doubt he had freed himself. No non-fisherman understands how real and bitter these tragedies are.

> The four of us caught sixty-seven salmon and grilse weighing 1,051 lb. Leaving out the grilse, our salmon averaged 18 lb., a heavy weight. In high water the spoon killed best, then the fly, sizes 6/0 to 2/0, and the prawn in a very low water. Large salmon have been taken, several over 50 lb. The English tenant of the water told me that every year he had experiences with these large fish: he had killed some, but they were difficult. They did not run up till late, when streams were low owing to the high ground being frozen. You had to fish a small fly and single gut: their mouths were smooth and slippery, and it was hard for the hook to take a good hold, and, if you did hook them, you had an hour's work in a river full of trees, snags and boulders. His best, if I recollect aright, was 55 lb.

The discretion that salmon anglers traditionally observed in those days is evident here, because we are not given the name of the 'English tenant' of the fisheries. Armed with that information, I might have been able to find out more and even document the full story of the capture of the 55lb Bardo or Malang salmon.

The only other reference, albeit a brief one, that I can find for a Malang or Bardo River salmon weighing 55lb is on page 87 in Ronald Swanson's *Record Atlantic Salmon* (Meadow Run Press, 2008), where the author notes a fish, 'Caught . . . by unknown Englishman prior to 1894.'

Doubtless a reader will be able to give me more help.

THE SALMON OF THE CENTURY – 55lb
No. 37

Patrick E. Chalmers is near the top of my list – as is doubtless the case with other anglers – of best angling authors. On pages 53–4 of *Where the Spring Salmon Run* (Philip Allan, 1931), he describes an incident that I believe happened on the North Esk – because a reader of the first volume of *Giant Salmon* told me it did. Incidentally, there is always an extra poignancy in relating stories of piscatorial derring-do if they happen on a river that is familiar to you.

> A relative of my own, upon an October afternoon and the light beginning to go, hooked a heavy salmon in a long, deep pool. He was fishing upon the

deeper side and under a high bank. He and his gillie knew the fish to be a big one. And I fancy (but they have never said) they imagined that it was a salmon of twenty-seven to thirty pounds who, as soon as he was hooked, sailed quietly inshore and along a ledge of rock just below the anglers. The fish was quite unhurried; I do not think that he yet realized that he was attached to the rod that bent in a hoop above him. So he came, nosing along the rock, deep down in the deep dark water. And as he came, Peter Maclellan [the gillie] stooped, buried the long-handled gaff in the water and drew the steel into him. And then all parties knew at once. There was a tremendous splashing, a tremendous lashing of a tremendous tail – 'God,' cried Peter to the angler, come awa', Sir, and gie's a hand wi' what's here!' So my relative laid down his rod and proceeded to Peter's assistance, and between them they had a fifty-five pound salmon on the bank within about three minutes of his taking the fly. I suppose that I, who have never caught a heavier salmon than thirty pounds, am envious of his good fortune when I say to the angler, as Mr. Stevenson said to Doctor John Brown anent the creation of the latter's Rab:

> Ye scarce deserved it, I'm afraid –
> You that had never learned the trade,
> But just some idle mornin' strayed
> Into the schule,
> An' picked the fiddle up an' played
> Like Neil himsel'
> Your e'e was gleg, your fingers dink;
> Ye didnae fash yoursel' to think,
> But wove, as fast as puss can wink,
> Your denty wab;
> Ye stapped your pen into the ink
> An' there was Rab!

Yes, Peter Maclellan just 'stapped' his gaff into the dark water and there was a salmon of a century, the spoil of an honest angler indeed but one who would as soon be playing bridge or golf as plootering in the river.

RICHARD ONSLOW'S
55lb ALTEN RIVER SALMON
No. 39

In July 2006, Richard Onslow was invited to fish the Sandia Beat on the Alten River by the Duke of Roxburghe. In the event, he caught the fish of a lifetime and was kind enough to write a thrilling account of the proceedings. This entry first appeared in the reprint of the first volume of *Giant Salmon*.

    The fish was hooked in Lower Dango at about 3 a.m. on 8 July. The water height was 1ft 6in. Odd and Agnar (the boatmen) had just told me to have one more cast from the boat, having fished through Upper Dango. We had drifted down into Lower Dango, and I was hand-lining in as the fly came on the dangle. The fly – a size 2 double-hooked and rather faded Munro Killer – was just under the surface a few yards from the boat when, moments before the fish took, there was a swirl in the water, which was only about a foot deep. At that time, we had no idea of the fish's size. It milled around for about a minute doing not a lot, and the boatmen started to row in to the side to land the fish.

    Then all hell broke loose: the fish surged downstream and I was nearly out of backing (about 300 yards) on my Hardy Perfect reel. I had to hold the drum on the left-hand side of the reel to try to add extra drag (I was also using my finger on the line to increase the drag). I shouted to the boatmen that I was about to be broken as my backing was nearly exhausted, and the boat set off downstream in pursuit of the fish. I was being completely carted.

    The fish stopped at the bottom of Gilvanista pool, which was about 500 yards from where it had been hooked. We had got within about 100 yards of it when it raced off down towards the Gilvo rapids, the top of the next beat. It stopped on the lip, just above the rapids. This was lucky as the boatmen said I would be broken on the sharp rocks if the fish went down. I reeled in as fast as I could, getting to within about 50 yards of the fish. At this stage, Agnar said that he would try to net the fish (which was nowhere near ready to be landed) off the boat as it was too dangerous to go down the rapids. Agnar dipped his landing net into the water and missed. The fish plunged straight down and went under the boat. It did this with such violence that the rod tip was also pulled under the water and under the boat! It swam towards the back and I yelled to Odd to lift up the engine before it cut the line. He did this just in time. I then saw both boatmen pulling on their life-jackets – they had seen the fish for the first time! The fish then tore off down the rapids, which were about 3ft high in places. 'Kneel down!' Agnar shouted. With the boat going down the rapids backwards, I managed to keep the line away from the rocks. At this stage, I thought it was only a matter of time before the fish was lost. It was still completely out of control. Miraculously, we managed to navigate the rapids with the fish still attached! We arrived in Gilvo pool (in the beat below) and moved the boat to the bank. The fish was still fighting hard in the pool, which was rather like a mill pond and very still, in complete contrast to the water we had just negotiated. About 20 minutes later, and a full 60 minutes after the fish had first been hooked, I gradually guided it towards the net. It was only at this stage that we realised what an enormous fish this was. It had travelled about 600 yards downstream in total. After three attempts, we managed to get the fish's head into the net and its body followed. It took three of us to lift it into the boat. There was nowhere suitable to beach it. Once in the boat, it flicked its tail and an oar shot over the side! It had been well hooked, with both hooks planted behind its tongue at the back of its mouth. It was a fresh cock of 55lb.

In a later letter, Mr Onslow indicated that the length of the fish was 50in and the girth 32in.

The 55-pounder, held by Richard Onslow, was the best fish caught by either of two rods in a total bag of 53 fish (grilse not included).

JEREMY BLOCH'S
56lb ALTEN RIVER SALMON
No. 40

Bozo Ivanovic, whose 50-pounder graces pages 79–81 of the first edition of *Giant Salmon*, gave me the particulars of another big fish, which was caught by his South African friend Jeremy Bloch. In March 2009 I received the letter below from Mr Bloch, and in April a few excellent photographs arrived.

I am fortunate enough to have a rod on the Alta in the first week of July. Last year, 2008, we arrived to find the river higher than anyone of the rods had ever known it. It was 6½ft when in a very high year it starts out at 4ft.

The first night before coffee I had a very hard time, touching 4 or 5 fish but not hooking any. After midnight, however, things changed and I caught a 28-pounder followed by a 45-pounder, followed by a 38 and a 38½-pounder.

But it was the third night that was the special one. My beat was Gonges to Vina Gorva (Vinakorva), and we started out in what Tormod, who is the most senior and respected boatman on Alta, felt would be the best pool – Vinakorva.

Because the river was so high, we fished lower down from the boat instead of wading as we normally do in this pool. The weather was pleasant with fluffy clouds, little wind and very few mosquitoes.

I was fishing with a Sun Ray Shadow, but made from colobus monkey fur, from a dead colobus that I found in Kenya.

Near the bottom of the run we rose a fish, but no touch. I changed fly and put on a Golden Jora. We covered the spot again but nothing moved. Tormod suggested that we move to another pool, but I just had a feeling and asked that we go back up and fish the bottom half of the run down again. We had a short break and I put back the Sun Ray Shadow and soon we were covering the water. The fly must have been two-thirds of the way round, when the whole fish came at least 6 inches out of the river. Tormod's son Kjetl, who was rowing in the front, saw it. I saw it. Tormod was behind me and didn't see it. The time was 9.15 p.m.

I resisted the temptation to jerk at the line, and waited for the heavy weight that I hoped would manifest itself at the end of it. I was not disappointed. Not a great deal happened to start with and I remember turning round to Tormod and saying, 'Tormod, this fish doesn't know it's been hooked!'

This photograph of JB's salmon is brilliantly composed. Hundreds of photographs are taken of big fish – only a few are as appealing as this one of JB with his 56-pounder.

Slowly, the Mosesons rowed up towards the bottom spit of Vinakorva, where there is a perfect place for landing a big fish. It was not to be. The fish came easily at first, but as we brought him near to the boat and the bank, he suddenly realised that something was amiss and he turned for the sea.

This first big run was down and across the river all the way to Kavala, about 300 yards. The analogy that I used in my fishing log book was that it "greyhounded like a Marlin". We were then able to catch up with it and a relatively shorter distance tussle ensued. We actually got the fish quite close to the net a couple of times, but the fish was having none of it, and decided it was time to head again for the salt. The first bit once again was like a marlin, but then it became just a steady movement and we were able to keep the distance from the fish fairly constant, as we both headed for Upper Sierra (Ovre Sierra) – a very famous Alta pool and the next place in the river where we could land a big fish.

We got there and gently led the salmon into the back eddy on the left bank, where we were able to net it. The time was 9.55 p.m. A fish of a lifetime!

ERNST DANILOFF'S
57lb 6oz ALTEN RIVER SALMON
No. 41

In July 2007 Ernst Daniloff caught his salmon on a Green Highlander tube fly in Langstilla Pool on Norway's Alten River. Although the fish looks the worse for wear – judging by the deep grooves in its shoulder – in all probability it had been entangled in a net (an estuary net?) before it freed itself and made its way upriver.

The fish having been bled shortly after capture, which is a Norwegian custom, Daniloff speculated that, had it been weighed straight away, instead of 12 hours later and after being bled, it might have been close to 63lb. I must thank the Norwegian newspapers *Altaposten* and *Finmark Dagblad* for the catch data, and David Hatwell for bringing them to my notice.

The happy Daniloffs with their dream fish.

JOHN H. DALSEGG'S
58lb 6oz SURNA RIVER SALMON
No. 43

Some of my correspondents go to great lengths to assist me in documenting the details of a salmon of which I had no previous knowledge. Such help came from Morten Harangen of Sandefjord in Norway, who was introduced to me by Peter Lapsley, editor of the *Flyfisher's Journal*. Morten wrote:

I have enclosed a postcard, that I believe I mentioned in an earlier or e-mail to you. It shows the biggest fish caught in the River Surna. As you may figure out from the back, this salmon weighed 26.5 kilos (58.3lb) and was caught in 1922 by Mr John H. Dalsegg. The gaffer was Peder A. Dønheim, and the girl on the photo is Gudrun Dønheim (possibly his daughter).

Morten couldn't provide details of the method used to catch this magnificent cock salmon and since he notes that 'further details about this fish are difficult to find', all I can do is speculate about the method used. Certainly, judging by the thickness of the butt section of the rod, it looks like a 20 or 22ft tonkin cane rod, beloved by some of the stronger fly fishermen in the nineteenth and early twentieth centuries – such a rod would be inordinately clumsy to

John Dalsegg's 58lb 6oz fish is probably the record rod-caught salmon from Norway's Surna River.

spin with. Coupled with the fact that Dalsegg is wearing waders, it seems to indicate that his method involved wading and casting with a big double-handed fly rod. The popularity of spinning for salmon had to wait for the development and availability of a reliable, lightweight multiplying reel, and/or a fixed-spool reel, which could be used in conjunction with a shorter rod of 9 to 12ft that could throw out a lightweight salmon spinning bait, such as a Devon minnow, with ease.

ULF-ARNE JUNGORD NILSEN'S 58lb 13½oz ALTEN RIVER SALMON
No. 45

Norway's spectacular big-fish river, the Alten, has produced yet another heavyweight. This one was caught on the Fiskeplasser beat by Ulf Nilsen on a Thunder and Lightning fly, and was reported in the Norwegian newspaper *Altenposten* on 7 August 2008. Ulf's father, Arnulf, who ultimately netted the salmon, told his son, when he eventually got his first glimpse of the fish, that 'this fish was no grilse'.

Of all the photographs of huge salmon that I have looked at, this one is the most unusual. It was given to me by Sir Edward Dashwood Bt after he had returned from fishing the Alten in July 2009.

The two men chased the salmon a long way down river in their boat, but eventually Arnulf jumped out in two feet of water, netted the fish over its nose and drew it ashore.* Doubtless the fish would have made more than the claimed weight had not the weighing been delayed for about six hours. The length of the salmon was 54in and the girth was 27in.

HOLGER LAUTH'S
58lb 9½oz EM RIVER SALMON
No. 46

Frodin's *Phatagorva*

By the time most copies of the first edition of this book were sold, I started to receive a steady trickle of new big-fish accounts, including a letter from a German reader, Dr Marcus Weyerke, who was able to provide details of two salmon that I had not come across before, one of which was Holger Lauth's huge autumn fish from the River Em, Sweden's most famous big-fish river (especially for sea trout). The other was Martin Hjelle's fish (see page 101).

Holger Lauth caught his salmon at 5.30 a.m. on 20 September 2008 on the Blackwater Pool, where he was Speycasting with a tube fly, the Phatagorva. The fish was 52½in long and had a girth of 29½in.

Since Herr Lauth is reluctant to send a copy of his photograph of the fish, I refer readers to that excellent German angling magazine *Blinker*. Their catch account is illustrated with this photograph.

---

* This method of landing a fish appears to be courting disaster – but it may be that my translation from the Norwegian newspaper will be found wanting.

Joyce Farrer's giant salmon, held by her gillie, Adolf.

SALMON BETWEEN 50 AND 60LB METHOD UNCERTAIN

JOYCE FARRER'S
50lb VEFSEN RIVER SALMON
No. 49

The existence of Joyce Farrer's giant salmon of 1934 was apparent after I wrote to her son Trevor Farrer about another 50-pounder that had been caught on the same river in Norway by a family friend J.W. Astley (see page 147).

This coincidence brings to mind another story of a lady involved in the taking of a 50lb salmon – reported by Thomas McGuane in his excellent book, *The Longest Silence* (Yellow Jersey Press, 1999).

> That night, I found myself dining with some English salmon anglers. One, a florid, lively man in his sixties, was telling me of the recent death of his mother who had always been bored by salmon fishing. On the Alta, where his father had persuaded her to fish for one day, she caught a fifty-pounder and never fished again. This year, as she lay on her deathbed, her son sat by her side. She was only occasionally conscious as her life ebbed away. At the end she opened her eyes and gazed at him. 'You'll never catch a fifty-pound salmon,' she said, and died.

Joyce Farrer in Föisjord

Joyce Farrer with the 50lb salmon she caught in the Vefsen in 1934, with the help of Adolf, her gillie, who was later shot by the Nazis.

A 51lb RIVER BLACKWATER SALMON
— No. 50 —

The first notice of this fish was listed in Notes on page 123 of the *Fishing Gazette*, 1 March 1890:

> The Irish Blackwater boasts the heaviest salmon of the year so far, viz., a splendid new spring fish of 51lb weight.

A more elaborate notice followed on page 130 of the same magazine under the Dublin correspondent's column Fishing Notes From Ireland, from which one assumes that it was rod-caught.

> The largest salmon I have heard of being killed since the season opened was one which was taken in the river Blackwater a couple days ago at the Lismore weir. The salmon was a splendid specimen of new spring fish and weighed 51lb. Some other fine ones landed in the lower waters, averaging from 20lb to 25lb. This looks well doesn't it?

LT COL. N.G. PEARSON'S 51½lb and 52lb NAMSEN RIVER SALMON
— Nos. 52 & 54 —

Lt Col. N.G. Pearson, sometime owner of the Gartland beat on the Namsen River, caught two salmon that qualify for entry in this book. This information was given to me in a letter from his grandson, the Reverend Nigel Pearson, who lives in Cambridge. The following note is an extract from that letter:

> In case it is of interest, two other over 50-pounders were caught by our family on the Namsen: my grandfather, the late Lt Col. N.G. Pearson caught a 52lb fish in the Kariol pool on 9th July 1930 (I may have a picture of him fishing in that pool that year, but need to check the pool) and he also caught a 51½lb fish in the pool on 9th July exactly two years later in 1932.

Lt Col. N.G. Pearson in July 1932. The largest of the three fish weighed 51½lb.

THE RECORD 52lb WELSH DEE SALMON
No. 53

Eric Hardy F.Z.S. wrote a piece for the October/December 1940 issue of *Angling*, about the salmon rivers of the north-west of England. This introductory paragraph sets the scene with some historical facts, before mention of a 52-pounder caught at Pickhill in 1779 and another big fish caught in 1899. Interestingly, he mentions the 82lb 14oz salmon that I featured in some detail (No. 460) in the first edition of *Giant Salmon*.

> Rod-fishing started on the Welsh Dee between the fourteenth and seventeenth centuries; coracle fishing with hand-nets, still practised in parts, was the original Dee method of catching salmon, while at Chester, especially at Handbridge, a number of men make a living net-fishing. The record salmon caught in the Dee was one of 52lb taken near Pickhill in 1779; one of 50lb was taken above Llandrino on June 10th, 1899, and one of 49lb near the same place on April 20th, 1895. A salmon of 82lb 14oz found on a stall in Manchester Market in 1881 may have come from the Dee, or from those other north-western salmon rivers (of the time): Mersey, Alt, Lune or Ribble.

SIR CHARLES BLOIS'S 52LB NAMSEN RIVER SALMON
— No. 55 —

Francis Francis, in his famous book *By Lake and River*, published by the Field Office (1874), records the story of Sir Charles Blois's 52lb salmon. He heard it from the man himself when he and a group of friends were fishing Scotland's Thurso River, in 1864 or thereabouts. That he was fishing with good friends is evident from the following observation:

> At breakfast next morning we all met together – six good men – the late Sir F. Sykes, the late Sir C. Blois, Col. P., Mr W., Mr D., and myself. What a jolly pleasant party we were! I never heard an angry or cross word the whole time I was there, and that is something to say, for I have heard brother anglers quarrel like Kilkenny cats, and use much worse language; but then our beats were so marked out that we couldn't conflict or collide in our fishing. We did not allow cards, and we never talked either religion or politics or philosophy, and eschewed all the ologies.

Thurso River (Beat No 8) where Francis Francis fished with his friends.

This is how Francis Francis recalled the story told by Sir Charles Blois.

> Sir Charles was an old Namsen fisher, having been one of the earliest of the British anglers who penetrated up the stupendous Fiskum Foss, pretty well known to a good many British anglers since then. He showed me on his gaff handle one day a notch which he had cut to measure the length of a big fish, that weighed either 52lb or 54lb (I forgot which), that he had killed in the big pool below the foss. He was in the boat by himself. He hooked the fish, rowed and managed the boat, and played the fish, landed, and gaffed him all by himself; and when the size of the fish is considered, that is a feat for anyone to be proud of. Sir Charles further told me that he hooked four other fish on the same morning, all as large or larger than the one he caught, and all of which he lost, chiefly for the want of a boatman; but he had a strong taste for fishing by himself, and could not bear to be looked at while fishing.

For the reference to Blois's fish I have to thank Roy Flury, who in turn is grateful for having received it from his friend, the Norwegian historian Per Gulbrandsen. I had to read some 377 pages of Francis's 418-page book before I found what I was looking for. Thank goodness it is such a fine book. Indeed, my friend the late Richard Walker loved Francis Francis's writing above all others.

THE HAMPSHIRE AVON'S LARGEST SALMON – 53lb
No. 56

Despite the fact that the Hampshire Avon has consistently produced large salmon, i.e. 30- and 40-pounders, the only 50-pounder that I am aware of was documented in Frank Buckland's *The Natural History of British Fishes* (Unwin, 1880).

A LARGE AVON (HANTS) SALMON

On Friday, April 2, 1880, a magnificent salmon was caught in the run of the river Avon (Hants) at Christchurch. It weighed 53lbs., and measured 4ft. 4½in. in length, by 2½ft. in girth, and was in most perfect condition. Mr. Tucker of Christchurch tells me that there is no record of any Christchurch salmon hitherto having been taken over 47lbs.; this fish I cast for Mr. Moss. I have also in my museum a cast painted by Mr. Searle, of a kelt salmon, 42lbs., also caught in the neighbouring river, Frome.

MR MYRAN'S 58lb 6oz NID RIVER SALMON
No. 63

In 1916, Mr Myran of Trondheim caught this magnificent fish in the Nid River in Norway. His grandson Oyvind Myran, who is presently (May 2010) in the Royal Norwegian Air Force, met up with Steve McPadden of Waldfeucht in Germany – gave him the particulars – together with the photograph of captor and fish.

Alas we do not know the method used to catch the fish nor do we know its length or girth – but judging from the photograph this fish was very heavily built. I dare say its girth would have exceeded 30 inches.

The River Nid runs into the Norwegian Sea, approximately one third of the way up the west coast of Norway (or two thirds down).

'Head of a 63-lb. Male Salmon, caught by the rod on the Tay, October 1907' from P.D. Malloch's Life History and Habits of the Salmon, Sea-trout and Other Freshwater Fish *(1910). No other details are given except for the details of the head which weighed 23lbs and the length of which from 'snout to gill cover' measured 15 in.*

SALMON OVER 60LB ANY METHOD

A MORAY FIRTH 60lb SALMON
— No. 65 —

The following announcement in the *Inverness Advertiser* appeared on Tuesday, 15 July 1856*:

> MONSTER SALMON.—On Tuesday last a salmon was taken in one of the nets at Chanonry Point, the largest that anybody can remember being caught in the Moray Firth. It weighed 60 lbs., was 4½ feet long, and 2½ in circumference. The breadth of the tail was 15 inches. We have this information from Mr Hugh Cameron, of the Chanonry Fishing Station, who had the good fortune to capture this gigantic fish.

If you look at a reasonably large-scale map you will see that Chanonry Point is the throat through which all salmon destined for the River Ness or the River Beauly have to pass.

Directly across the water from Chanonry Point is the village of Ardersier. At the time of the capture of the 60lb salmon in 1856, Ardersier had a thriving fishing community. Many families in the village depended on the sea to earn a living. The Reverend John Mathieson, a Victorian minister, wrote a history of the parish that included some interesting observations about the fishers:

> ... a class of people who possess many habits and many superstitious observations quite peculiar to themselves. They never intermarry out of their own tribes, and there is an obvious reason for this on the part of the young men, as no other females would undertake the laborious out-of-door occupations to which their wives are subjected. They carry in creels on their back to great distances immense loads of fish: and they carry their husbands to and from their boats, when from the state of the tide, they cannot get in or out dry-shod. This latter duty influences the fashion of the costume of the females, which, as regards their lower garment, is of peculiar brevity. The women make the nets and bait the lines, and the fishermen when not employed on the vasty deep, do little else than chew tobacco.

* A bigger fish (84lb) is said to have been caught in the Moray Firth (see Giant Salmon No. 464).

This photograph of Chanonry Point was taken from high ground on the north shore of the Moray Firth – notice the white lighthouse on the point.

This extraordinary photograph shows fisherwomen carrying their menfolk to and from the boats on their backs, as described by the Reverend John Mathieson.

A SEVERN 60-POUNDER?
No. 66

Since this fish had been killed by, and provided a meal for, an otter, we can be sure that prior to that it weighed in excess of 60lb. It was 1 inch longer than another Severn salmon, the 64-pounder caught by Thomas Allen in 1912 (*Giant Salmon* No. 165).

The following extract appeared in the *Fishing Gazette* on 4 January 1890:

A BIG SEVERN SALMON

Mr. William Darling, superintendent water bailiff for the Severn Board of Conservators, found at the confluence of the Severn and the Rhiw in Montgomeryshire, recently a male salmon which had been killed by an otter. The only marks on it were a bite in the back and one in the head. The weight of the fish was 58½lb: it was 4ft. 6in. in length, 2ft. in girth at the broadest part. It was in prime condition. This is the largest fish which has been seen in this country for many years.

Otter devouring a salmon, from a drawing by Edwin Landseer, RA.

MARTIN HJELLE'S
60lb 14oz EIDS RIVER SALMON
No. 67

Dr Marcus Weyerke from Germany, having read the first edition of *Giant Salmon*, wrote to my publisher with news of a fish caught in Norway in May 1944, during the last war, at a time when information about Norwegian fishing was not generally available. The fish was caught on the Eids river at Eidselva, close to the Stryn river, which is well known for big fish. A brochure promoting the fishing at Eidselva describes how Martin Hjelle took his brother Knut with him to fish the Hammar Pool with unbelievable

The photograph of Hjelle's 60lb 14oz hen salmon, although technically of poor quality, is nevertheless outstanding in that it truly conveys the size and perfect shape of the fish. Notice the angler's hand where it grips the dorsal fin.

success when, after a long battle, Knut was able to net what turned out to be the heaviest hen fish ever taken on rod and line. In his letter, Dr Weyerke quotes details taken from the brochure:

> Experts came from Oslo to do tests, take measurements and weigh the salmon. The salmon proved to be 7 years old and had she not been caught would have spawned for the third time. The weight of the fish (two days after she was caught) was 27.6kg i.e. 60lb 14oz. The length was 129cm i.e. 50¾ins, and the girth about 80cm i.e. 31½ins.

A NEAR RECORD ENGLISH SALMON FROM THE BORDER ESK
No. 68

On pages 420–23 of *Giant Salmon* I described the finding of a monster kelt, said, when fresh-run, to have weighed between 70 and 80lb in the Border Esk at Netherby, which was reported in a letter to the *Fishing Gazette* on 2 February 1907.

I heard nothing more about this fish until 2 November 2009 when I received a letter from Bruce Latimer, enclosing an old cutting from a local newspaper with details of a 62lb salmon:

> I just bought your salmon book. On page 420 you have an entry for a monster kelt from the Border Esk. I enclose an old cutting which may have some relevance to this, or not.
>
> The cutting is from around 50 years ago when I was around 12 years old. Unfortunately it is not dated on the page. It is from the pink sports paper, which I think was the *Cumberland News*, then published on Saturdays and my father took in those days before television probably.
>
> If the year is correct, then the 1902 given would be different from your 1907.
>
> The Border Esk is my home river and along with the Liddle, which forms the border for much of its length, is the only river I've fished much for game fish.
>
> Funnily enough, I had never visited Kirk Andrews on Esk until this year, when I was fortunate enough to be let in by a couple of elderly lady

volunteers who were about to lock up the church. The church is in fact Church of England and that side of the river is in England, too. The church has some river bank and fishing rights attached, they said.

To return to the 62lb salmon, I suspect this is the same fish. Unfortunately the one-armed man has his hand over its 'kype'. I think it could be a kelt in reasonable condition. If it was a kelt and killed by the fisherman, it was nearly back to the Solway and if it returned again, might have been even more massive! However, it would have had to negotiate the myriad stake nets which then formed a veritable forest on the Solway.

To return to the cutting, 'John Elliot' [nickname 'Popple'] would be the then editor of the *Eskdale and Liddlesdale Advertiser* (the Langholm newspaper) which is still in existence and has been taken over by the Cumberland News Group.

The following is a copy of the extract culled from the *Cumberland News* or one of the newspapers mentioned above:

Near Record Salmon from Esk?
This 62-Pounder is a Mystery

Hard on the heels of last week's article about Britain's record game fish comes news of a 62lb salmon – not, I hasten to add, caught recently, but at least captured this century.

Writing from Langholm, Mr John Elliot tells me that I appear to have created something of a controversy among local anglers there because I omitted to mention the fact that this huge salmon had been caught from the Border Esk in 1902.

This, however, is not surprising – as it is the first I have heard of it. And the record books contain no reference to it either.

Mr Elliot writes: *'A few weeks ago this old photograph was unearthed and interested Esk anglers no end. It was taken in 1902 and shows the record salmon taken with rod and line from the Esk – 62lb. The photograph also shows the successful angler (central figure) and the stipulated two witnesses. The monster was caught by the late Andrew Johnstone, Hagg Knowe, Long-town, Cumberland, and thereby hangs a tale.*

'Can this fish be termed a Scottish salmon, or is it a "Sassenach" specimen as it was caught in that portion of the river as it flows through Cumberland on its way to the Solway?'

Bruce Latimer may well be right in suspecting that there is a connection between the dead kelt of the Fishing Gazette report and Mr Johnstone's 62-pounder; so now I have a puzzle that I hope a reader can help me solve.

One look at the picture should convince everybody that this is certainly a big salmon. But did it weigh 62lb? I tried to find out.

English Record

Mr Johnstone and his partner are obviously tall men – six-footers, I would say. Working on this assumption, the salmon appears to be approximately 54 inches long. A quick glance at the weight-for-length ratio tables and my calculation makes this fish well over the 60lb mark.

Now, if this salmon did weigh 62lb, and if it was caught fairly with rod and line – and I am in no position to question the angling methods employed by the late Mr Johnstone – then it is definitely the heaviest taken from an

English river, beating the 60-pounder captured from the Eden in 1888.

At 62lb it would also be the second biggest salmon taken from any British water this century, being only two pounds lighter than the 64-pounder caught in the Tay in 1922.

Many more details are required, however. There is just the chance that somebody in Langholm may remember this salmon. If they do, I'd certainly like to hear from them.

Just before publication Bruce Latimer sent the author the above photograph, with the following note: 'According to Sir James Grahame Bart of Netherby Tower, the fish was landed in the section of river shown above, i.e. north of Netherby Suspension Bridge.'

A 63lb MONTROSE MONSTER
No. 70

On 21 June 1890, the *Fishing Gazette* published details of a huge cock salmon that was netted at Montrose. Since the town lies on a spit of land between the North Esk and the South Esk, it is impossible to say which of these rivers the fish was about to run before it was caught.

MR. T.R. SACHS called on us to say that Mr. Groves, of New Bond Street, on Monday last received from Melrose-on-Tweed a fine salmon of 63lb. Mr. Henry Ffennell went with him to see the fish, and very carefully took its measurements. Mr. Ffennell kindly supplies us with these particulars: - "Dear Mr. Marston – With very great pleasure I send you particulars of the large Scotch salmon which I weighed and measured in Mr. Groves' shop in Bond Street yesterday. It was a very handsome male fish, and turned the scale at 63lb. It measured from tip of snout to middle of tail 55in., and in girth the tape showed 29in. Mr. Dennis, the obliging manager of Mr. Groves, bought the fish from Messrs. Forbes, Stuart and Co., of Billingsgate, to whom it was consigned. It was taken in the nets at Montrose, and I think we may conclude it was a North or South Esk fish. It was by a long way the best salmon, both as to weight and condition, that has reached London so far this season. Last week Mr. Dennis sent me particulars of a fine Tay salmon he received from Mr. Speedie, of Perth. I was out of town, so could not weigh or measure the fish myself; but I think we may confidently rely on the following particulars which Mr. Dennis kindly sent me: - weight, 54½lb; length, 52in.; girth, 28½in. I understand this fish was also in fine condition, bright in colour, and fresh-run from the sea."

Henry Ffennell, as readers of *Giant Salmon* will be aware, made it his duty to respond to stories about large salmon, and whenever possible, personally inspect, weigh and measure the fish. In this way, over the years, he managed to expose quite a number of fraudulent claims and scotch a number of speculative reports.

A 66lb 2oz NAMSEN RIVER SALMON
No. 72

In the first volume of *Giant Salmon* there is an entry (No. 413) for a 68lb salmon caught on the Namsen River in 1931 by Fridgeir Sagmo. A model of this fish was on view in a sports shop near Grong, and I used a photograph of this model to illustrate the entry. In June 2009, Dr Roy Flury showed me a copy of the book *Namsen I Våre Minner* in which a brief mention of the fish appears together with the same illustration of the carved salmon seen in the Grong sports shop. However, a second photograph is also included, showing a framed picture standing on a table. This photograph within a photograph depicts three men clustered round a salmon that has just been landed. Although an enlargement of the framed photograph proved, as expected, to be extremely grainy, it caused me to consider that it might prove to be one of the greatest photographs ever taken of a giant salmon – if only we could have access to the original framed print and have it copied and enlarged.

Fortunately, I was able to correspond with Morten Harangen – fisherman of Sandefjord in Norway, and master of at least two languages. Here is my letter to Morten, dated 22 July 2009:

The magazine article intrigues me, although I can hardly understand any of it. However the framed photograph being held by Fridgeir Sagmo is stunning. The way the three participants, viz. Fridgeir Sagmo, Johan Williksen and Inge Sagmo, are standing or kneeling with the fish being held so as to offer its full side or flank to the photographer, couldn't have been better arranged – not even by a highly-skilled professional photographer.

The photograph, despite being taken with a simple box camera, must rank as one of the finest, if not the finest, big salmon photographs ever taken. This leads me to ask many questions.

What is the name of the journal that published the article and when was it published? Presumably Fridgeir is dead – do we know when he died and who is now in possession of the framed photograph? If we had these data to hand together with a copy of the original framed photograph, it would make a fine chapter for Volume 2 of *Giant Salmon*, planned for publication in October 2010.

Here 76-year-old Fridgeir Sagmo holds a framed photograph of his fish.

I look forward to your opinion of the chances of locating the framed photograph and the chances of getting a new photograph taken of it.

Knowing that I had put Morten on the spot, as it were, I was absolutely delighted when I received the following letter from him.

I found it! Here is the photo of Fridgeir Sagmo's famous salmon, caught on May 28th 1931. One of his daughters had the original, and you have her permission to use it in your book.

Now, the details:

It was caught on the Namsen beat belonging to Holandsøya gård (Holandsøya farm, Grong municipality), more precisely at Reve, downstream of the Brautahølen (Brauta pool).

As I mentioned in a previous letter, the fish wasn't weighed until the next day. Then, it was exactly 30 kilos (66lb). I've spoken to Jon Ivar Moe, who lives at Holandsøya today. His father, Oluf Moe (then 7 years old), remembered the extraordinary catch very well. According to him, the weight was 30.9 kilos (68lb). Sadly, the old catch records, once kept at the farm, seem to be lost.

What I do know, however, is that Fridgeir Sagmo was born on April

12th 1905. He died on February 26th 1985. His daughter told me that he usually fished with spoons, so I assume his 1931 salmon was caught on a spoon as well.

The photograph, depicting a huge Namsen salmon that weighed 30 kilos (66lb 2oz) a day after it was captured, although it was estimated to have weighed 68lb when it was caught, is without doubt a piece of angling history.

The finely composed 80-year-old photograph of Sagmo's salmon.

A 68½ lb FIRTH OF FORTH SALMON
No. 73

In March 2009 the editor of *Trout & Salmon* telephoned me to tell me of a call he had received from Hugh Newton. Having read the first edition of *Giant Salmon*, Mr Newton wondered if he (or I) would be interested to hear about a huge kelt that had been caught in 1871 by professional fishermen in the Firth of Forth.

It turned out that Mr Newton remembered seeing the mounted head of this fish in Edinburgh's National Museum of Scotland when he visited it in 1964. Wisely, Mr Newton had checked with the museum that the head was still in existence before contacting the editor of *Trout & Salmon*. The weight of the fish before it spawned had been estimated – presumably by a member, or members, of the netting team – and recorded as 84lb.

Geoff Swinney, the head zoological curator of the museum, gave me the accession number of the item and kindly agreed to have the fish head photographed on my behalf. The records reveal that the Edinburgh firm of John Jameson (fishmonger's) had given the fish's head to the museum and that it was caught in August 1871.

It is interesting that the record tells us the fish was netted in the month of August in the Firth of Tay (i.e. in salt water), and that it was described as a kelt. It could only have been a kelt if it was a survivor of the 1870 run of spawning salmon – in which case it must have spawned in the winter of 1870/71 and then dropped back to sea.

My sums tell me that this fish had been a kelt for 8 or 9 months, that it had suffered an estimated weight loss of 15½lb and that it was soon to die, but that's all. However, the existence of the fish does draw attention to the fact that we know little about the number, or the size, or the sex of kelts that are caught in salt water by professional netsmen, because there is no incentive for them to keep records and it is illegal for them to kill such fish.

Furthermore, we shall never know in which river, out of all the rivers that run into the Firth of Forth, this monster completed its spawning act, although the Leven, the Forth and the Devon are among the favourites.

The mounted salmon head (accession No. NM52-1872-13A) is on view in Edinburgh's National Museum of Scotland in Chamber Street. If some of the fish's scales have survived the taxidermist's beheading cut, it might be possible to read the age of the fish, and even observe the spawning mark.

THE LARGEST RHINE SALMON CAPTURED ON CAMERA – 69lb
No. 74

This book has many references to large Rhine salmon, as well as an acknowledgement that, if the truth be known, the Rhine has almost certainly produced more giant salmon than any other river in the Northern Hemisphere. The photograph on the right, taken from Werner Bocking's book *So We Fished on the Lower Rhine: Images of an Ancient Craft* (Kleve Boss, 1989), shows a 69lb Rhine salmon. Sadly, all the catches are ancient history, since the river suffered from persistent and growing pollution when it became the main drain for unwanted poisons as Europe's Industrial Revolution grew.

All the reports that I possess of giant salmon from Germany have been about commercially caught fish, and what follows is a typical example. On 8 June 1902 *The London Globe* published a note from their correspondent Mr Henry Ffennell about a large salmon. It is interesting to record that such notes, if they documented German fish, were always about Rhine salmon, whereas if they originated from, say, Norway, the rivers, if specified, were one of a dozen or so that held big fish.

> **Some Big Salmon.**
> From The London Globe.
> Commenting on the remarkable trio of salmon which has just reached this country from Norway, Mr. H. Ffennell gives the dimensions of three Rhine salmon which were brought to England in 1889, and formed a trio hardly less notable. The three from Norway weigh together 157½ pounds, the biggest turning the scale at 56 pounds and measuring 48½ inches by 28½ inches, the next weighing 55½ pounds, and measuring 51 inches by 29 inches, and the third weighing 46 pounds, with a length of 48 inches and a girth of 26 inches. Of the Rhine salmon, the heaviest nearly turned the scale at 55 pounds, and measured 51¼ inches by 28 inches. The larger of the two other fish scaled just 4½ ounces under the 50 pounds, measured 47¼ inches in length and 27½ inches in girth, while the other salmon was 6 ounces under the 50 pounds, and measured 47 inches by 27 inches.

Werner Bocking, from whose book the photograph on the right is taken, wrote extensively about the history of the Rhine – especially about its shipping.

A 70lb 8oz
FAROESE SALMON
—— No. 76 ——

It is not in the remit of this book to study the progress of all the organizations who have fought for decades to safeguard the future of *Salmo salar*, but Derek Mills' excellent book *Saving Scotland's Salmon* (Medlar Press, 2009) does exactly that and more.

In 1980 it came to light that a floating long-line salmon fishery existed off the Faroe Islands, with an annual catch that had just risen to 536 tonnes. Long-lining is a traditional method used by professional fishermen, both at sea and in freshwater, in order to catch fish that feed on or near the bottom – rather than pelagic species that feed in mid-water or near the surface in open waters.

For the latter kind of fishing, the Faroese had developed a floating long line, consisting of a series of manageable sections called pins, where each pin is made up of some eighty 12-foot lengths of nylon, traditionally known as snoods. Each snood is fitted at mid-point with an appropriately sized barrel lead, and has an eyed hook baited with a sprat at the business end. Snoods are attached to the mainline at regular intervals by means of a swivel. The mainline is buoyed up to the surface with plastic floats that are attached midway between the snoods. In practice, twenty-five joined-up pins would make a long line of 18 miles. Such lines are deadly when fished at night or in rough seas. When Derek Mills first visited one of the Faroese processing plants in 1982, he noticed that the line-caught salmon were particularly large, some in the 40lb category, and the largest weighed 70½lb.

Since 2009, and as a result of considerable diplomacy and goodwill, the Faroese and Greenlanders – with suitable compensation – no longer fish for salmon on the high seas.

A 71lb 6oz
SULDAL RIVER SALMON
—— No. 77 ——

Feast your eyes on a fish that would fulfil a fisherman's dream. It weighed 71lb 6oz, was 52¾in long and its girth measured 33in. It needed two men to lift it off the ground. The photograph was given to me by the ever-helpful Sir Edward Dashwood Bt, managing director of Churchill Gunmakers, based in High Wycombe. Details of the fish were given to Sir Edward by Christian Bjelland, whose father and grandfather had a lifetime's fishing on

Two employees of Christian Bjelland can only just shoulder the salmon, so as to lift its kyped underjaw off the ground.

Norway's Suldal River. Although the family have kept records, this fish, caught in June 1952, had 'slipped though the net' – an expression that hardly seemed appropriate when Christian guessed that the salmon was caught in a 'kilenet' (which, I believe, is similar to the Scottish bag net). However, he concedes that it could have been caught on rod and line.

The following description of a bag net comes from Derek Mills's *Scotland's King of Fish* (William Blackwood, 1980), a book that is crammed with fascinating information about *Salmo salar*:

> The bag net is commonly used on rocky coasts and consists essentially of a trap made of netting to which fish are directed by a leader, that is, a line of netting placed across the route the salmon usually follow as they move along the coast. The salmon swim towards the leader but cannot get through and instinctively turn seawards. Swimming along the leader they are led into the mouth of the net and through a succession of compartments into a final chamber, or fish court.

THE COXENS OF TWICKENHAM AND THEIR RECORD 72½lb THAMES SALMON
No. 78

T.R. Sachs, a long-time member of the Piscatorial Society, frequently had articles and letters published in the angling press. On 6 July 1883, the *Fishing Gazette* published the following letter:

LARGE THAMES SALMON

SIR – In looking over my album of fishing events, I came across the following, which I noted at the time: Richard Coxen, fisherman of Twickenham, and three others, caught a salmon of 72½lb. in 1820, and sold it to Watkins of Bond Street, for 8s. 6d. per lb.

This was related to me and other friends by Richard Coxen in 1860; he was then about seventy years of age, and lived to be eighty. He was the most truthful, honest, and obliging fisherman I ever knew, and much respected by all his angling customers. Many a time self and friends have had tea and Thames flounders at his cottage, near the river – it was a speciality there. Once I remember the Piscatorials had a match for the heaviest of fish caught at Twickenham. Mr. Francis Francis was my partner; we were victorious, and enjoyed the excellent dinner provided by Mr. and Mrs. R. Coxen, which the other competitors paid for. I might here mention that Mr. Francis Francis gleaned a life-store of information respecting the Thames salmon from Richard Coxen, long before I knew him. The late old John Keene and John Harris told me, more than thirty years ago, of their exploits with the Thames salmon, when they saw one leaping, "as they always do," out went the nets and the fish was captured.

This bust of Francis Francis (sometime fishing editor of The Field*) is a plaster copy of the original that is on view in Winchester Cathedral.*

I have several times assisted in putting thousands of Buckland and Ponder's salmon fry in the Thames at Moulsey, Sunbury, etc., but nothing much came of them. The college students at Sunbury used to amuse themselves in catching them with the fly at the tail of Sunbury Weir. A few skeggers, or two-year-old salmon, have also been caught at various places lower down. Mr. Greville Ffennell published in *The Field* some few years back, an extract from the diary of the keeper of Boulter's Lock, "not far from Maidenhead," giving the number and weights of salmon caught at the weir there, year after year, till the catch came to nothing.

A salmon weighing 23lb. was caught on April 19, 1870 at Gravesend, by a whitebait fisher. The fish was bought by my late friend, Frank Buckland, and who kindly presented me with a nicely-painted cast of same. My late friend fondly hoped it was one of his, returning home again; but at last came to the conclusion that it was a stray salmon. They are occasionally, even now, caught in the Medway. I am, &c.

T.R. SACHS

Editor R.B. Marston added the following comments:

> The filth and traffic below Westminster bridge are the greatest impediments to salmon coming up the Thames. They come every year to the mouth of the river but turn up their aristocratic noses at Barking's tribute.

From Samuel and Anna Hall's classic *The Book of the Thames* (1859), we learn that during and after the latter part of the eighteenth century, the village of Twickenham was a fashionable choice for London notables to build homes for their retirement. Nearby Eel Pie Island was used by picnic parties for obvious reasons. As we observe from Sach's letter, tea and Thames' flounders, offered to him and Francis Francis by Richard Coxon, were another local speciality.

In 1829, nine years after Richard Coxen and his team caught the largest Thames salmon ever recorded, Thomas Falkner's book *Historical and Topographical Description of Chelsea and its Environs* was published. The book gives an interesting historical background to some aspects of professional salmon netting in the River Thames as early as the reign of Charles II.

> Salmon fishing on the Thames begins on the 25th of March above London Bridge, and ends the 4th of September. They (the salmon), bear a most extravagant price in the London markets, having been sold at 12s. a pound; 8s and half a guinea a pound is frequently given for the whole fish together,

and the average price is 5s, although the quality is probably equalled in other rivers, and there is so little other excellence in the fish beyond their being caught so near the Metropolis, and not losing their flavour by long carriage before they are brought to table. To be eaten in perfection, salmon cannot be too fresh.

Most readers will have noticed reports that Thames salmon always fetched the highest price on the London market, leaving them with the impression that Thames salmon were somehow superior to other salmon, whereas Falkner tells us that the real reason was the closeness to the market in London, which assured their freshness. This, of course, was in the days before refrigeration.

Mr. Falkner also gives an interesting account of the salmon fishing at Chelsea. He says: "It appears by authentic documents that in the reign of Charles II the fishing was carried on here to a very considerable extent by Charles Cheyne, Esq., the Lord of the Manor, and others, but owing to the evil practices of the fishermen in using unlawful nets and from other causes it fell into decay, and finally proved an unprofitable speculation. The right of fishing extended from Battersea to Lambeth. About the year 1664 Sir Walter St. John resigned all his rights to the "rooms" of the salmon fishery with the river Thames to the fishermen of Chelsea, between Upper Lindsay Place above the Feathers, towards the west to the creek called York Place Creek on the east, with free liberty to cast and draw up their nets upon part of the waste adjoining, and also to the departure and liberty to feed one horse upon the waste for drawing up the fishing boats, and on the same year a bond was drawn up between the following mentioned persons, viz., Charles Cheyne, Esq. Joseph Alstone, John Saunders, Edward Cox, Daniel Burt, and John Colson, who paid the sum of £84 into the hands of John Burgess and John Wild for the half of four salmon nets, which were to be employed yearly in the several fishing rooms of Chelsea and Lambeth during the season, and the conditions were that they should keep the nets in repair, and weekly during the season make a just account of all profits arising from the fishery by equal proportions to the above-named Charles Cheyne, Esq., and partners at the dwelling-house of John Colson, in Chelsea. On Monday the 30th of May, 1664, the Chelsea fishermen began to fish, and took from Monday to Saturday nine salmon, weighing 172½lb, and sold them."

On 1 September 1883, approximately 50 years after the last Thames salmon was caught, a river report in the *Fishing Gazette* for the previous week's fishing at Twickenham names three fishermen with the surname Coxen – James, George and Richard. Presumably, these professional boatmen were descendants of the team that netted the 72½lb salmon in 1820. Alfred Perrin, who sent the report, indicated that all forty of his punts were let out, and he advised early booking to avoid disappointment!

Several famous angling authors have lived or worked in Twickenham, including Hofland, author of Hofland's *British Anglers Manuel* (1839), Francis Francis, author of many books, including *A Book on Angling* (1867), and Sir John Hawkins, who prefaced the early life of Izaak Walton in the 1760 edition of *The Compleat Angler*.

The Thames at Twickenham: the river here features the famous 'deep', all 150 yards of it, opposite the villa and grounds once owned by Alexander Pope (1688–1744).

This photograph of the channel between Eel Pie Island and the town of Twickenham also shows the pillared walkway behind which are the tearooms, stretching along the left-hand side of the river, that have served anglers and boating people for centuries. Moored close to the high embankment (remember this is tidal water) are two fishing punts, each equipped with a pair of ryepecks (iron-shod poles) that are driven into the mud, so as to anchor the punt across a chosen swim in the river. The design of these punts has changed little since Queen Victoria's reign – the only concession to modernity is the outboard motor. A few yards upstream is the bridge that gives free access to the famous island.

THE 72lb 12oz SULDAL RIVER SALMON
No. 79

In May 2009 Sir Edward Dashwood and I discussed the possibility of his, through his Norwegian friends, producing photographs of huge salmon of which I had previously been unaware. The first fish – a veritable monster, weighing 72lb 12oz – was netted by a 'kilenet' in the fjord just outside the mouth of the Suldal River on 30 May 1947. The length was 56¼in and the girth 31¾in. This information, together with the photograph of the fish, was kindly provided by Sir Edward's friend, Christian Bjelland.

Giske Pedersen Foldøy stands next to the fish, outside the premises of Christian Bjelland & Co, so as to demonstrate the scale by which we can judge the size of the salmon.

MR GRIEG'S 75lb
SAND RIVER SALMON
No. 80

Mr Grieg's gravitas reflects the attitude of many successful British anglers in those times, which was to resist the temptation to look pleased at having caught such a huge fish. He has probably asked his gillie to look the other way so as to hide his smiling face.

In March 2008 I received a letter from expatriate Welshman Lew Watts, who now lives in the USA.

> I have just read, cover to cover and with great pleasure your *Domesday Book of Giant Salmon* and was prompted to write to you about one large Norwegian salmon which does not appear, but has been documented.

As you will see from my address, I live in Washington DC but am originally from Cardiff, in Wales, and 'cut my teeth' salmon fishing on the rivers Wye and Usk. In the early 1980s I was fortunate to live in Norway for several years and, since that time, have returned each year to fish many of the rivers from the far North (Tana) to the south (Vosso, Sand, Ardal and Tengs). I do this with my closest friend, Lief Inge Andersen, who first mentioned the large salmon caught in Sand River in the Suldal Valley.

On 5 March 2008 Leif Inge Andersen sent an email to Lew Watts in which he had translated a text written in 'New Norwegian' into English.

The largest salmon caught in Suldalslaagen weighed 75lb (34kg). It was caught by an Englishman named Mr Grieg in 1913. He fished below Sandsfossen in a boat together with his gillie Tolliev Swensen who came from Sand. They hooked a salmon and the salmon pulled the boat and both of them onto the fjord and inwards towards Sauda, all the way to Tangen, which is 10km from the estuary of Suldalslaagen. Here the salmon turned around and was soon on his way back to Sand. Here the two men went ashore at Einersneset and had some food before the salmon was landed. They had been in the boat for 12 hours. We have full documentation of this salmon and attach a photo of it.

A 76¼lb SALMON FROM THE RIVER DEE
No. 81

At the moment, an oil painting featuring a 76¼lb Dee salmon seems to be all that we know about a fish that was caught in 1875. From the comprehensive cracking of the paint, it looks likely that the painting was executed soon after the fish was caught. However, it is unusual to find a remarkably good painting surviving so long without the catch details being recorded. We don't even know in which River Dee it was caught.

'The Salmon (Salmo salar) 76lb 4oz Caught in the Dee 1875.' *The design of the painting is very much like the layout beloved of nineteenth-century taxidermists, who used weeds and stones to decorate the interior of a glass-fronted case on which they painted the legend in gold lettering edged with black enamel.*

AN 82lb 10oz SALMON FROM ALTEN FJORD
— No. 82 —

In the first week of July 2008, this huge fish was caught in a bend-net on the Alten Fjord, at a time when big fish in the Alten system would normally have already moved up into the river. The report was first published in *Altaposten* and then again, on 5 July 2008, by Harold Oyen in *Fish Norway*. The netsmen were Egil Olai Bårdsen and Dagfinn Nicolaysen. A local fishmonger, who gave up the chance to buy the fish, stressed that it would be better if it were smoked.

Ivar Leinan, director of the Alta River Association, is reported to have said that it would have been a difficult fish to land had it been hooked, and pointed out that such a huge cock fish would be nothing but trouble on the redds, because big fish are so aggressive and spend most of their time chasing away other males rather than getting down to business.

The editor of *Fish Norway*, Colin Bradshaw, made an excellent suggestion when he wrote, 'Wouldn't it be even better if the fish had been radio tagged, returned, and its progress monitored,' adding, 'Is it not time to pay netsmen to do this?'

This view of Alten Fjord, looking out from Bossekop, reveals a ring of snow-capped mountains (in July) with some form of hanging or drying rack in the foreground.

THE 102½lb
NEMEN ESTUARY SALMON
—— No. 83 ——

Notice of this fish is available on the internet (www.worldrecords.com/salmon), where it is described as having been caught in 1860 by 'other methods', (presumably in a net), at the mouth of the River Nemen in Lithuania. It weighed 46.5kg, i.e. 102½lb.

Reference to the map below will reveal the huge catchment area of the River Nemen, which rises just 20 miles from Minsk in Belarus. It flows into the Baltic near Klaipeda in Lithuania, a distance of some 250 miles as the crow flies and probably nearer 400 miles on the ground.

When a dam was built in Kaunas in 1959, the tributaries of the Nemen/Nemunas River below the dam retained their good runs of Baltic salmon, but because the hydro installation did not include a fish-pass, salmon could no longer continue their migration upstream.

Whether sport fishing has been allowed to develop since Lithuania regained its independence, I do not know; but with such a big river the scope must be enormous both for salmon and trout fishing. The future looks good in the wake of the resurgence of herring and sprat populations in the Baltic, since these are the salmon's principle fodder fish.

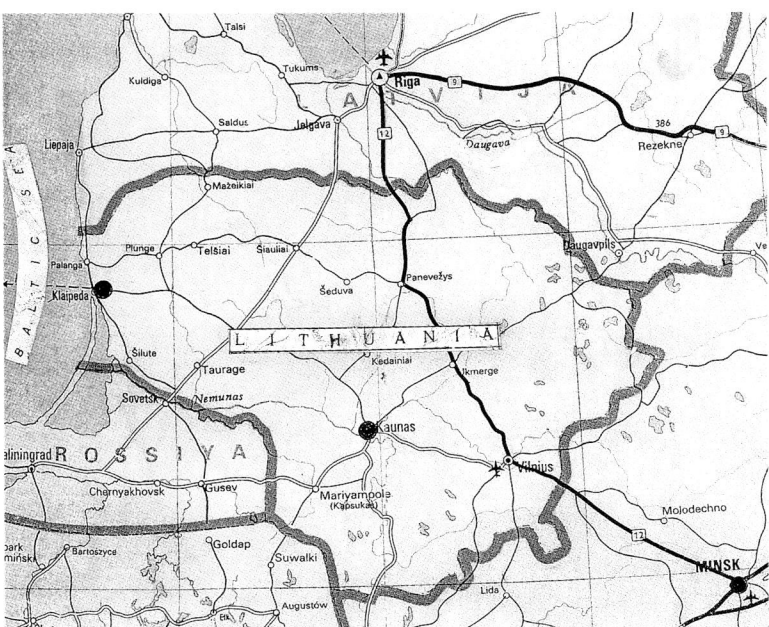

A POACHER'S 109lb HOPE ESTUARY SALMON
—— No. 84 ——

Where will you find more beautiful scenery? You may find it in other parts of Sutherland or Argyllshire, but views of the east side of the Kyle of Tongue will take some beating. (A kyle is a narrow strait or sound.)

In September 1978, *Trout & Salmon* published a letter from Dr Paul Riley, a retired GP from Scunthorpe, which contained the following note.

> A patient of mine, an ex-poacher, caught a male salmon of 109lb in the estuary of the River Hope in a 'hang net' in September 1960. It was weighed at a farm near Tongue and then sent to the Continent with others.

Sadly, Dr Riley was unable to remember the name of the patient, who had moved from Tongue to Scunthorpe after he retired. This entry first appeared in the reprint of the first volume of *Giant Salmon*.

In late August 2009, having been flooded off an Upper Scone beat on the River Tay, my wife and I drove north to Tongue, with the intention of investigating the story of this enormous fish. In the event, when I arrived, I was lucky enough to see Jonathan

Straw, a most helpful salmon fisherman whom I had once met at the Flyfishers' Club. He gave me the name of the keeper of the Hope Fishery, who operated from Hope Lodge, which is located at the head of the river by the loch's outflow. Having made details of my mission clear to the keeper, Ian McDonald, he responded by saying that although he had no personal knowledge of the 109lb salmon that was netted in the estuary, he had heard others speak of it, and he was pretty sure that the fish was weighed at Tongue Mains Farm, located on the east side of the Kyle of Tongue, on land that was once owned by Clan Mackay, but was now owned by the Countess of Sutherland.

Thanks to Jonathan Straw, I planned to meet another local man, who was said to possess a fund of local knowledge, namely Alick Mackay, better known as Alick George, who lives in the scattered village of Talmine. His house was difficult to locate, since the houses were not numbered in the conventional fashion but in a chronological sequence depending on the date when each crofter was allocated his land.

Before I got into deep conversation with Alick Mackay, I needed to know why he was known locally as Alick George. His answer was that there were so many Mackays in the district that his second Christian name made for certain identification. Alick George

Tongue Mains Farm where the fish was weighed.

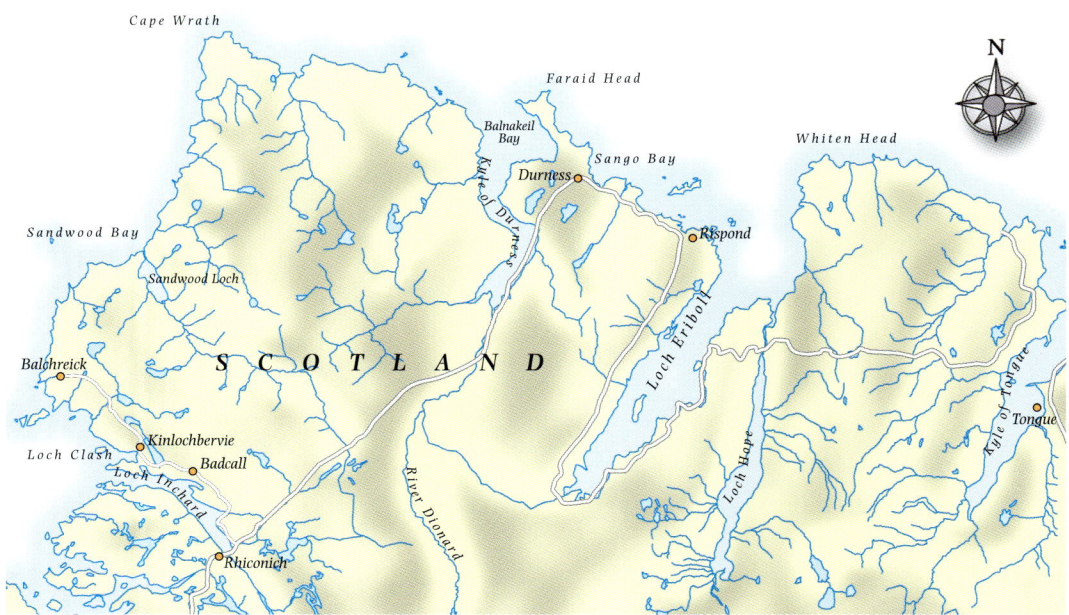

A map showing Loch Eriboll and the Hope estuary where the 109lb salmon was caught.

Mackay remembered little about the story of the big salmon other than the fact that yet another member of the Mackay family had caught it.

He also remembered that a local poet had written a song about the monster salmon but alas, due to the passage of time (nearly 50 years), he couldn't remember it. Interestingly, I learned from the keeper that netting of salmon in the estuary has ceased entirely.

In the absence of any recorded evidence, I believe that two points need consideration. The first is that we can dismiss any connection between such a large fish and the River Hope, as really big fish are invariably associated with certain big-fish rivers (that are either large or turbulent or both), the names of which are scattered throughout the pages of this book.

The second point is a geographical one. Although we know that Atlantic salmon, when they are ready, navigate from their Greenland and Icelandic feeding grounds towards their home river, the following extract from *Falkus and Buller's Freshwater Fishing* (Stanley Paul 1988) tells us how they do it:

> Recapture of tagged fish indicates that salmon returning to Britain move in from the Atlantic at many points, swimming close inshore up or down the coast until they reach their river estuaries. Although a small percentage (Nature's insurance policy) find their way into strange rivers, the majority

return to spawn in the rivers of their birth. It is not known exactly how a salmon navigates from the distant ocean to the coast, although recent research suggests that a magnetic indicator in the front of the head is mainly responsible; but experiments have established beyond doubt that it selects its parent river by the particular odour of that river. Salmon have an almost unbelievably acute sense of smell.

From the above it is clear that, because of its size, the Hope estuary salmon, if it existed, would have been the leader of a shoal of salmon crossing the Hope estuary in the course of navigating round Loch Eriboll sea loch (see map). Its fatal mistake was swimming into the poacher's net. We shall never know the name of its natal stream – it could be hundreds of miles away, and sadly the only person who knew whether it was swimming up or down the coast (in this case west or east) was its captor.

Loch Eriboll, looking north-east from the western shore. Rispond, a village overlooking the far north-western end of Eriboll, was home to salmon fishermen and workers in a salmon-processing station (which included a boiling house) that served the whole of north-west Scotland until it ceased trading in the early twentieth century. An excellent account of the history of this fishery and its fishermen is to be found in Andrew Graham-Stewart's brilliant book, The Salmon Rivers of the North Highlands and the Outer Hebrides. *(Robert Hale, 2005.)*

The mouth of the River Ewe with Pool House Lodge opposite in about 1900.

ADDENDA TO VOLUME I

The grand Ewe salmon and its captor.

MORE ABOUT KEEPER GRANT'S 50lb RIVER EWE SALMON
Vol. 1 No. 4

In September 2009 I received a letter from Mr and Mrs Armishaw, proprietors of the bookshop River Reads in Torrington, Devon, enclosing a cutting taken from the *Fishing Gazette*. They had just purchased a batch of angling books and found it tucked into one of them. The cutting was a letter from Henry Ffennell to the editor and included a photograph of the fish that was missing when I featured the catch (No. 4) in the first volume of *Giant Salmon*.

THE LARGEST ROD SALMON OF 1902

DEAR MARSTON – I have much pleasure in sending you a photograph of a salmon, which I think was, without doubt, the largest taken by an angler in our home waters during the season of 1902. You may like to figure it in the *Fishing Gazette*. The photograph was kindly forwarded to me by Mr. John Dugdale, KC, on whose water on the River Ewe, at Poolewe, Ross-shire, the fish in question was landed in June last. It weighed 50lb and was a male in splendid condition, fresh from the sea, and was captured with a fly by the keeper, Osgood Grant.

This salmon was seen coming in from the sea on June 15th in company with another very large fish, and was caught on the 16th. The other fish was not taken. In the previous year a salmon of 40lb was landed in the same river, and was an exceptionally large one for the River Ewe.

I am sure you will agree with me that the photograph gives great credit to Miss Joan Dugdale, a young lady aged ten. It was taken in front of Mr. Dugdale's house in Poolewe. The captor Osgood Grant holds the fish in his arms, and I think the pair represent two as grand specimens as one would wish to see.

Yours truly,
Henry Ffennell

Henry Ffennell kept readers informed about catches of very large salmon but was always careful to vet the claims before he passed on any information. Ffennell had already had a list of big salmon published in the *Fishing Gazette* on 3 May 1902 (see page 205) but the above data reached him too late for inclusion.

Perhaps we shall never know what induced Osgood Grant to hold the fish upside down. However, the photograph, now that it is being made public for the second time, may bring forth a letter of explanation. A catch account would also be of great interest.

MORE ON LETTICE WARD'S 50lb RIVER TAY SALMON
Vol. 1 No. 13

Thanks to my friend Keith Elliott, editor of *Classic Angling*, in June 2008 I received a photograph of Lettice Ward with her 50lb Tay salmon (No. 13 in Vol. 1) plus an account of the capture taken from the *Fishing Gazette* of 20 October 1928.

LADY ANGLER'S FINE 50LB TAY SALMON

We have pleasure in giving a reproduction of an excellent photograph taken by Mr C.D. Geddes, photographer, Perth, and showing Miss Lettice Ward with her 50lb salmon, which she caught last Friday in the River Tay.

The fish put up a strong resistance of fully 1½ hours before being brought to gaff. Length 51¾ in., girth 27½in. Miss Ward is a niece of the Hon. Sir John Ward, Kinnaird House, Ballinling.

We congratulate Miss Ward on her success in landing a fish equalling in weight the heaviest fish caught on the Tay this season. This was killed on July 10 by Major Frank Pullar, and according to Mr Hutton's reading of the scales it was a six-year-old large spring fish. The photograph shows Miss Ward's big salmon to be a typical autumn cock fish.

Miss Lettice Ward with her 50lb salmon, caught with a 4/0 'Kate' fly in the Alderns Stream, River Tay, on 12 October 1928.

W.G. CRAVEN'S RECORD 53lb SPEY SALMON
Vol. 1 No. 77

In March 2008 I received the following letter from Algernon Perrey, the great-great-grandson of W.G. Craven, whose fish is No.77 in *Giant Salmon* Vol 1:

> I thought you might like to see the enclosed copy of a photograph of Mr Craven's 53-pounder, caught on the Spey on 4 October 1897. Mr Craven, my great great grandfather, is on the left. The 'clipper' [gaffer] is Mr W. Davidson.
>
> I had a model made of this fish two years ago by Ronnie Glass of Kelso, using the measurements detailed in our fishing book. The model is now in Fochabers, Morayshire.

Mr Craven (left) with his gillie Mr W. Davidson and the suspended 53-pounder.

FRED MILBURN'S
PERFECT 54lb SHANNON SALMON
Vol. 1 No. 97

If it were in my power to award a prize for a photograph of the most beautifully proportioned salmon that I have ever seen, then I would choose Fred Milburn's fish, because this salmon is near perfect. I recorded all I knew about it in the first volume of *Giant Salmon* (No. 97) after finding details in the *Fishing Gazette* of 14 November 1903 and the *Daily Mail* of 4 September 1904. Then in December 2009 I discovered another account in the *Fishing Gazette* (17 March 1903, page 166) in the form of a letter from Henry Ffennell (who was a serious big-fish researcher) to the editor.

CAPTURE OF THE 54LB SHANNON FISH

My Dear Marston – I send you a photograph of the 54lb salmon taken by an angler on the Shannon. It was kindly forwarded to me by Mr F.C. Vansittart, a keen fisherman and a prominent member of the Limerick Board of Conservators. You will observe that it was a very handsome fish, and you may perhaps like to figure it in the *Fishing Gazette*. It was landed by a Mr F. Milburn, on Feb 14th, on the famous Dooness fishery. The measurements were length 50in, girth 30in. The weight and measurements were verified by competent persons in Mrs Enwright's well-known hotel at Castleconnell. The fish was in splendid condition, fresh-run, with sea-lice adhering. I see it is stated in some papers that this fish was the largest salmon landed by rod and line in Irish waters. Such, however, is not the case. In 1872 a salmon of 58lb was taken by an angler on the Shannon, and in 1874 one was landed by a professional fisherman, Michael Maher, at Longfield on the River Suir in Tipperary.

To return to the Shannon salmon fisheries, I regret to learn that the conservators of the district continue to be much troubled at the manner in which magistrates' decisions as to illegal fishing are dealt with by the authorities at Dublin Castle.

Yours always

Henry Ffennell

Although the subject of the sex of Milburn's fish was not raised, it looks as though it was a hen fish, since there is no visible kype. I have seen many items used as background when attempts are made to photograph a fish – a bed sheet hanging on a clothes line, or on a door, appears to be one of the popular choices. In this photograph, a rowing boat seat or a shelving board has been pressed into service.

ESMOND BRADLEY MARTIN'S 55½lb GRAND CASCAPEDIA SALMON
Vol. 1 No. 123

In February 2008 Jorge Sanchez of Palm Beach, Florida, who is Esmond Bradley Martin's son-in law, wrote to me about his father-in-law's catch (Vol 1 No. 123).

Among the papers sent to me by Jorge Sanchez was a piece written by Esmond Bradley Martin, let's call him EBM, describing his capture of the record fish, which was published by the *Atlantic Salmon Journal* (No. 1, March 1959). The account was included in an article entitled 'Record Atlantic Salmon' by Carnes Weeks M.D., and although somewhat idiosyncratic, it is beautifully written and deserves to be better known. EBM entered his fish in the Field and Stream contest and won an award, but at the time he couldn't bring himself to write an account of the combat between himself and the fish simply because there was no combat – due to the superb skill of his guide, Collie Gideon, who had gaffed the fish in record time.

> I was twenty-four when I was invited to fish the New Derreen waters by Mrs Frederick Guest, my aunt, in 1939. I remember very well what took place on June 27th of that year. I had a standing offer to give one of my guides $100 if we succeeded in landing a record fish.
>
> On the 27th of June, 1939, I was fishing in what is called the upper

EBM's salmon, skilfully preserved and mounted by a taxidermist so as not to reveal the gaff damage that was noticed and treated on the bank with consummate skill, 'carefully stuffing the gaff wound with grass to prevent loss of weight'.

Esmond Bradley Martin, his 55½lb fish and his two guides, Collie Gideon and Lorney Willett. EBM caught a salmon weighing over 40lb earlier in the day.

water (top third) of the Derreen waters at Maple Pool, just above a broad, lengthy stretch of water called Limestone. We had finished with Limestone and I had already caught, this day, my first salmon weighing over forty pounds. We had poled upstream and moved over to the far side of Maple to start fishing on this pool. It was fairly late on a beautiful sunny day. The pool isn't remarkable for anything, except that the monster was caught in it. It is outclassed in every way by Limestone which is productive (or at least was) in high or low water. Limestone is a very appealing place to fish, Maple is nothing to look at. The river at this place is relatively narrow. Three-fourths of the width of the river is shallow and useless. On the far side (on the opposite side of the river from the road and camps) is a fairly deep run with about a dozen very large boulders, widely spaced. Although I call it a run, the water doesn't move very fast, nothing like Jack the Sailor, for instance; there are no whitecaps as the rocks are well below the surface. I doubt if a stranger would ever think of fishing this spot. It is a small pool, never used for spawning, of course, and only worth fishing during the spring runs and high water. I think it is very unlikely that salmon stay in this pool for any length of time, as they obviously do in many of the more famous pools on this river. It is, however, the only pool where the salmon may rest between Limestone some distance down river and a pool called '424' upstream, also at quite a distance.

    I never liked this place and jokingly told my guide that he would never get his $100 here. Fortunately Collie Gideon, my head guide, paid no attention to my remark and we set about trying to raise something. I was using a medium-weight short greased line rod, multiplying reel, cheap, heavy synthetic leader a 'D' iron Lady Amherst fly. I believe a 'D' iron is the same as a long shank 8/0, but I am not sure. Collie is, I know, the best fisherman who ever was on the river. His main thesis is that his boat cannot catch anything by staying off the river! Fish, fish, fish was his creed and, as a result, I always did relatively well. He used to try every type of fly and every size, no matter what the season. I think I was the first to try greased line fishing on this river and I was not popular with him during these efforts. The system worked very well, but he never accustomed himself to the small size of the fly. He had used the same casting technique for years, though. As a matter of fact, he used every technique and, if a fish were ever raised, that ended it, we were there for the remainder of the day, although several resting times interrupted our efforts to trick this unfortunate fish. Things were going along smoothly, nothing exciting, though I did see some fish in the pool, which I considered surprising. Suddenly the huge thing rose out of the depths in a slow gigantic surge of silver and white, turned and made off with the fly. I never have been in a mood to toy with my fish. I derived most of my pleasure from seeing the strike, anyway, and my equipment was strong enough, or so I thought, to play the canoe, in comparison with my dry fly outfit. The fish stormed off, the anchor was hauled in and we drifted with the current.

    There was no need to follow the fish or worry about its actions. There were no underwater logs or roots or sharp rocks, etc. ... The fish rose to the surface once or twice, revealing its size to Collie but not to me. I had never seen a fifty-pounder alive and could scarcely hope that this was a record. Besides this, I have never been able to estimate accurately a fish on the end of my line, the way others can or say they can!! In about five minutes Collie decided to take matters in his own hands, poled out into midstream and, when the giant surfaced once again, he found himself at one end of a pole! No nonsense about paddling to shallow water or waiting for the fish to tire! In these instances, Collie is made of stern stuff and will brook no unnecessary delay to earn his prize! We hauled him in and found our scale was useless, the miserable tool only weighed to fifty pounds! Carefully, stuffing the gaff wound with grass to prevent loss of weight, we left off our fishing and rushed to camp to weigh our fish. It weighed fifty-five and one-half pounds. As a matter of fact, it weighed fifty-five and one-half pounds so often on its trip to New York, that the poor fish was permanently elongated and slightly the worse for wear, necessitating papier-mache reproductions! To add to its indignity, the taxidermist mistook it for a western species and put a curve in its back!

MISS WHEEN'S 57lb NAMSEN RIVER SALMON
Vol. 1 No. 135

Although I was unable to include a photograph of Miss Wheen's 57lb salmon in my account of her catch in the first volume of *Giant Salmon* (No. 135), I am now able to show a picture of her brother Richard's best fish, which he caught in 1896.

Richard Wheen's huge salmon (extreme right), although not dignified by a specific weight, looks to be well over 50lb when compared to the height of the gillie, Jorgen Strande.

MORE ON G.B. BAINBRIDGE'S 57½lb NAMSEN RIVER SALMON
Vol. 1 No. 143

Some months after the publication of the first volume of *Giant Salmon*, Adrian Bradley told me that, somewhere in his loft, he had a photograph of a Victorian angler with a massive salmon. Then, in September 2008, came the good news that he had found the missing photograph, which he enclosed with his letter. 'I look forward to hearing your opinion of the angler and the fish,' he wrote. 'I have wondered for years who he was and where the fish came from.'

The 'loft' photograph shows Mr Bainbridge holding the fly-rod and reel that was used to catch his fish.

The photograph was of G.B. Bainbridge with his Namsen salmon (Vol. 1 No. 143) – printed from a broken photographic glass plate – and it is different from the one already in my possession. I daresay that Mr Bradley was surprised to discover that Mr Bainbridge caught his fish in 1937. Doubtless the latter's classic sportsman's clothes, which owe nothing to fashion, fooled him into thinking that the fish was caught in Victorian times.

PERCY TARBUTT'S 58½lb EIRA RIVER SALMON
Vol. 1 No. 151

Although Percy Tarbutt's fish appeared in *Giant Salmon* Vol 1 (No. 151), the account was pieced together using a number of different reports, and details of its capture were scanty.

It was not until April 2008, when I received a note together with a circa 1935 Ogden Smith catalogue from my friend David Burnett, that I was able to make further progress. The weight was given as 58¼lb, and the fish was taken on fly using a 12-ft Ogden Smith 'Warrior' salmon fly rod.

Although we can deduce that Percy Tarbutt was a shy man, because he did not allow Ogden Smith to use his name to promote their tackle in the catalogue, he nevertheless allowed his modified version of the rod to be marketed as the 'P.C.T. Warrior Salmon Rod'.

Peter Prag, in his *Salmon and Sea Trout Fishing in Norway* (1953), gives the weight of Tarbutt's fish as 55¼lb and quotes *Where to Fish* (1952) page 305 as his reference. From the same source we had already learned that the length of the fish was 51in and the girth 29¼in.

However some 15 months after the publication of *Giant Salmon* in 2007, I received a letter from Percy Tarbutt's granddaughter, Belinda Martin. Later she sent a clear glossy print of the original photograph of Tarbutt and his fish, together with his own notes on the capture, which I am bound to regard as definitive. It was a 6¼-year-old unspawned cock fish, weighing 58½lb, length 48½in, girth 28½in, condition factor 45.2, caught in the Eira River in 1931.

MAJOR IVAR HAUGE'S 70LB TANA RIVER SALMON
Vol. 1 No. 169

This fish was recorded in the first volume of *Giant Salmon* (No. 169), noting that it was first documented in Philip Kingsland Crowe's book *Out of the Mainstream* (1970), on page 89, although it was not illustrated. Recently, my friend David Hatwell located a photograph depicting models of what he understands are the Major's two biggest salmon. The larger one is the 70lb Tana fish that he caught in 1952, and the other is one about which we know nothing except its weight – 50lb. Both models are on view in a fisherman's lodge on the bank of the Tana River, possibly at Levajok Fjellstue, part of which was Major Ivar Hauge's fishing camp.

DR ALEXANDER LINDSAY'S 51½lb RIVER TOWY SALMON
Vol. 1 No. 172

Soon after the publication of the first volume of *Giant Salmon* (October 2007), I received a letter from Douglas Evans of Carmarthen with more details of Dr Lindsay's fish (No. 172) which, when pursued, led to my moving its entry from the No. 2 list, where the method was classified as uncertain, to the No. 1 list, 'Caught on Fly'. Dr Lindsay caught his fish at Abercothi on the River Towy and, interestingly, although Jack Hughes-Parry recorded a weight of 50lb in his book A *Salmon Fisher's Notebook, A Fishing Fantasy* (1949), Mr Cyril Fox of the Abercothi Fishery records a weight of 51½lb. In his letter to me of 18 February 2008, Mr Fox confirms that the fish was taken on fly.

Dr Lindsay with his salmon. A model was made of the fish, presumably with accurately taken measurements, and from that (courtesy of the Abercothi Estate Fishery) we can deduce that the length was 50in and the depth 11½in.

The Record Pool at Abercothi, where Dr Lindsay caught his fish.

J.W. ASTLEY'S
50lb VEFSEN RIVER SALMON
Vol. 1 No. 180

Malcolm Thorne, a noted collector of pictorial artefacts, bought the damaged wood carving from Mr Jones and had it repaired and re-photographed.

Following the publication of the first volume of *Giant Salmon* in 2007, I received a telephone call from Hugh Whittam of Ulverston in Cumbria, giving me a lot more information on a fish that was already recorded in my lists (No. 180) but with minimum detail.

His friend B. Jones, also from Ulverston, possessed the woodcarving of this fish caught by J.W. Astley in the Foss Pool at Fossford on the River Vefsen in Norway on 14 June 1919. He suggested that I write to Trevor Farrer C.B.E., who had probably owned the carving at one time. My letter to Mr Farrer elicited the following reply:

> I have some information about salmon fishing on the Vefsen in Norway. My grandfather first took a stretch of the river in about 1906 and he and my father fished it every year (except 1914/18) until 1939. They had a house built near the river, which the Germans burnt down when they retreated from Norway. My father, William Maurice Farrer, fished the river from 1922 and my grandfather, William Farrer, died in the fishing house in 1924.
>
> Amongst those who regularly went were the Astley brothers (JW, J and F) and Sam Whymper* (brother to Edward, who first climbed the Matterhorn). Sam was game manager to Lord Curzon, Viceroy of India, and shot 98 tigers – many of them for preying on villagers.

---

* One of the Whymper brothers caught a 53-pounder (No. 258).

My father's best catch was a 60-pounder, but he and others often caught half-a-dozen fish in a day over 30lbs. My mother, with some assistance from her gillie Adolf, caught a 50-pounder. They sometimes fished from the bank, sometimes harling from boats; sometimes with fly, sometimes spinning.

Trevor Farrer's letter revealed the connection between his family and the Astleys, and as a consequence nicely tidied up the incomplete entry No. 180. However, his letter also revealed the existence of two more giant salmon – his mother's 50-pounder (see page 86) and his father's 60-pounder. Both entries could be linked to entry No. 334 in the first volume of *Giant Salmon*, which previously accounted for three different fish.

MAJOR PULLAR'S 50lb RIVER TAY SALMON
Vol. 1 No. 185

Major Pullar's 50-pounder

Since the publication of the first volume of *Giant Salmon* there has been a constant flow of new information from readers. Malcolm Thorne, an avid collector of angling memorabilia, sent a splendid photograph of Major Frank Pullar's salmon (No. 185) to my friend David Hatwell, which was duly passed on to me. The legend revealed that the Major's fish was caught on 10 July 1928 in Upper Eel Brig pool on the Stobhall beat. The fish was beautifully mounted by P.D. Malloch of Perth, who also noted on a small plaque, located in the bottom right-hand corner of the case, that it was a cock fish, aged 5½ years, and was taken on a size 2/0 Dusty Miller fly.

The information that came to me via Malcolm Thorne allows me to move the Major's fish from List 2 (method uncertain) to List 1 (caught on fly). A mention in the *Perthshire Advertiser* of 18 July 1928 has also come to light:

A Beauty from the Tay

One of the best salmon caught for many years was landed from Lower Stobhall water by Major Frank Pullar, of Bridge of Allan. It was a magnificent male fish of fifty lbs. and measured 50¼ inches in length and 26¼ inches in girth. The successful fly was a 3/0 Dusty Miller, and the fish made a long run, taking out 150 yards of line at its first rush. Despite this, however, Major Pullar landed the fish after half-an-hour's play. It is rare for such a big salmon to be caught in the Tay in July with the rod. It must be stated that this was a newly run fish, with sea lice adhered to its sides.

'51½ lbs. Killed by W.F. McDonnell at Castleconnell 18th May, 1928.' This photograph of John Tully's carving of McDonnell's Shannon salmon (No. 217) is superb. Notice that the legend on the mounting board declares the weight to be 51½lb, but I prefer to recognize the stated weight at time of capture, which was 51lb.

McDONNELL – THE MIX-UP AND THE MASQUERADE
Vol. 1 Nos. 216 and 217

If readers care to consult pages 38–9 in the first volume of *Giant Salmon*, they will see two consecutive entries for a 51lb Shannon salmon. The first (No. 216), according to an entry in *The Big Fish* (Oglesby and Money-Coutts, 1992), was caught in the spring of 1928 by F. McDonnell, whereas Major W. McDonnell (No. 217), according to Jock Scott in Game Fish Records (1936), caught his fish in 1929. Naturally, I was suspicious that an error, or errors, had occurred in the documentation of one or both of these fish, but I had no proof to justify dismissing either claim.

A letter dated 4 March 2008 from Charles Carroll of Drogheda, near Dublin City was able to put me on the right track:

> I enjoyed your book on giant salmon very much. Seeing as you must have quite an archive on these fish, I thought you might like some more information on the fish of 51lbs caught on the Woodlands beat of the Shannon at Castleconnell in 1928.
>
> A carved wood model (done by Tully's) of this magnificent fish was on display at the far end of Garnett and Keegan's, which was the premier fishing-tackle shop in Dublin for many years. As a boy, I was always

The Doonass Water at Castleconnell on the Shannon before the river flow was reduced by the hydro-electric scheme. In 1923 the Reverend Joseph Adams wrote: 'It is a miniature Niagara from World's End to Landscape. Above the falls and below them the Shannon is raging mad, racing, leaping, seething, foaming like a thing possessed.'

fascinated by it and used to ask about it when my father was buying tackle. It had been owned by the famous fisherman, author and judge T.C. Kingsmill Moore, author of *A Man May Fish!* Very regretfully, the business got into financial difficulties and went bust many years ago. I happened to know the accountant who acted as receiver and managed to buy the fish when all the assets were being disposed of.

I managed to track down quite a bit of information about it, including a report in the *Fishing Gazette* of the fish with details on scale-readings made of it at the time. I also have a photograph from an old edition of *Trout & Salmon* showing the fish, gillie and captor. You may well have seen the reference to its capture in the Lonsdale Library edition of *Salmon Fishing*, which includes a chapter on Castleconnell by John Rennie. Tantalizingly, he referred to the 'epic struggle, which would take too long to tell in this chapter'! It is such a pity because from the reference, there was clearly a great battle. The chapter by Rennie does however give a great feel for the difficulty those anglers faced in handling a big fish in the days of the old Castleconnell water height. [See Appendix No. 26.]

In due course, Charles Carroll provided me with a copy of an editorial note culled from the *Fishing Gazette* of 26 May 1928, reporting John Enright and Son's letter regarding the capture of a 51lb salmon on 18 May 1928, and the details of a scale reading (giving the age of the fish) that followed, in a letter from J. Arthur Hutton.

A Fine 51lb. Shannon Fish

Although the 53lb. Salmon caught by Mr. R. de Bohun Devereux in the Wye is, we believe, the heaviest salmon caught this season, the River Shannon is a long way ahead of other salmon rivers in the British Isles for the number of heavy fish that have been killed during the 1928 spring season. Here are particulars from Messrs John Enright and Son, of Castleconnell, of a splendid fish, and also a report from Mr. J. Arthur Hutton on the scales.

DEAR SIR – We enclose some scales from a fine fish killed here yesterday on the Woodlands Cut by Mr. W.F. McDonnell. Length 52 inches, girth 28 inches, weight 51lb. We would be obliged if you would have the scales read for us.

Mr. McDonnell, fishing odd days has had some very good sport, getting amongst others, three 34lb, three 35lb, one 38lb, one 40lb, and the big one yesterday.

Thanking you in anticipation, yours sincerely
JOHN ENRIGHT AND SON

Shannon May 18 – 51lb., 52in. length, 28in. girth: presumably a cock fish. Two years in river, four years in sea: a very large spring fish, which had not spawned. The scales are slightly disintegrated, showing that the fish was beginning to lose condition, as is often the case with spring fish at this time of the year. The condition factor was barely 36½.

My original suspicions were well founded. The above details, given to the *Fishing Gazette* within a week of the fish's capture, must be taken as gospel, so the year of capture listed in Jock Scott's Game Fish Records some years later, and consequently recorded in the first edition of *Giant Salmon* as 1929, must be incorrect. Furthermore, when I read Doonass's article in conjunction with the above, and looked at the pictured carving of Major McDonnell's fish, it became clear that Doonass's fish must have been caught in the 1928 season, at the latest, and that the fish caught by Major McDonnell in May 1928 (as the legend shows) were, in fact, the same fish. There was only one fish weighing 51lb and it was caught in May 1928 by Major W.F. McDonnell, who masqueraded as Doonass when he described the battle to land what was probably one of the last* Shannon monsters to be caught on rod and line. Doonass's account underlines the validity of John Rennie's description of killing this particular fish as an 'epic struggle'. Here is his epic account, published 23 February 1929 in the *Fishing Gazette* in a piece entitled 'The Devil's Own Luck'. Doonass had taken his pen name from that famous big-fish beat on the Shannon, and he described how he caught what could prove to be one of the last 50-pounders ever caught on that river.

> I had rented a well-known water on the Shannon at Castleconnell, but with business engagements I could only get away for the week-ends and it necessitated a drive of some eighty odd miles. This meant I was lucky when I got to the river about 4 o'clock on Saturday afternoons.
>
> This particular Saturday, in the middle of May, appeared a perfect fishing day; I was a bit late in starting, and it was 5 o'clock when I arrived on the river. My two boatmen, Bill and John, were waiting, rods mounted and keen to be at it. As I stepped into the boat, Bill suggested I had better bring my coat, and pointing to the hills, remarked. 'You will need it very soon.' In my hurry I had not noticed that the weather had changed completely. There was a deluge approaching, and without hesitation I said, 'We had better stay where we were, and get shelter under some pine trees close by.' With this the men agreed, and in less than five minutes came distant rumbling of thunder, and along with it rain came down in torrents. For over an hour it continued, and indeed I had almost despaired of throwing a line when the rain began to get lighter, and in another ten minutes it had practically ceased.
>
> Needless to say, during all this time we had been carefully watching the river which at this point was over one hundred and fifty yards wide, but not a fish showed.
>
> It was now close on 6 o'clock when we got into the boat. I must own my hopes of success had fallen considerably. Same were still further damped after fishing our first pool. A perfect piece of smooth water, lying at the tail of some turbulent and broken stretch of water just above it with rock showing here and there. It was in good order for a fly, but nothing showed, and it was with some misgiving I agreed to Bill's suggestion to leave it and try the pool higher up with a shrimp.
>
> This necessitated putting me ashore while they poled the boat up the

---

*Two other 50-pounders were caught in 1928 – M. Tuohy's 50lb fish and D. Slattery's 50½lb fish. Liam Ford's 50½lb fish in 1933 was probably the last.

rapids. I could not help feeling that in doing so I was making a mistake. The run I was now about to fish was in the main a stream, and very rapid. It was only about 10 yards long, just above the turbulent stretch, and although it bore a great reputation I had never had any success in it.

The previous week I had hooked a good fish there, but failed to hold him when he dashed down-stream taking out some sixty or seventy yards of line. Before we could follow he had broken the line.

The men now had some difficulty holding the boat in this heavy, rapid-running broken water. However, Bill was still full of hope, for it seems that while waiting my arrival he had seen a couple of good fish show, and only mentioned it as I started fishing with a very short line in an eddy at the top. I was beginning to think I had fished the best of it when the shrimp was taken with "a snap" and the next instant the reel was screaming. The fish had hooked himself, and was rushing up-stream away from the boat. Before he had gone more than ten yards he showed in a flying leap clean out of the water. 'He's a huge one, boys,' I shouted (for the noise of the water was deafening). 'This line will never hold him.' Neither of them had seen the fish jump, because seeing the fish rush up-stream, both immediately started poling the boat up for all they were worth, keeping parallel with him. Next instant our fish was rushing towards us, and it was fortunate that the weight of water kept a good strain on the line, while I recovered it as hard as I could.

Within five yards of the boat he stopped, and Bill implored me to try and hold him as short and as hard as possible.

For four or five minutes I managed to do so, notwithstanding the fact that more than once he got the top of my rod under water. However, he was not to be denied, and in a flash he had turned, and before I could do anything he was dashing straight down-stream in the middle of the heavy water out of the run.

'Get after him! Get after him!' I shouted. Seconds passed. It seemed ages to me. The line was flying, and I had lost touch with the fish. Three or four big rocks, a foot or so out of the water, lay apparently right in our path, and, with rod bent double, I completely lost sight of his direction as the boat dropped back. Bill, in the stern, could not look round, and, with the point of the rod straight over his head, he kept shouting to me not to let him go too far, and also to know at which side of the rocks the fish had gone. Not being able to see properly, I could only respond, 'Let her back! Let her back as quickly as you can!' Next moment the boat sheered a little, and I was able to see that our fish was right away down, and very close to the head of the pool where we had started, and still going down-stream.

Bill, on hearing this, at once stopped trying to hold up the boat, and let her race for the next fifty yards. I was reeling for all I was worth, trying to keep strain on the line as the boat shot back safely to the lower pool. Now I felt our fish was fairly safe. I had succeeded in recovering the line, and, as we were within a few yards of the fish, I was in a position to fight him under favourable conditions. The river below us was for some four hundred yards a smooth sheet of water, and a couple of hundred yards wide, with a few rocks showing on the surface. Immediately I put on some strain, away went our fish towards some shallows on the south bank. 'Get after him! Get after him!' and the men lost no time over doing so. Next moment our fish had turned, and was dashing for the opposite bank. 'Hold him, sir, hold him! He will break you round that rock in the middle of the river.'

'Hold him be damned!' as the rod was doubled right up with the strain. 'Get after him! Get after him!' I shouted. 'I can't hold him!' and the fish had again got away with some fifty yards of line.

Working like Trojans, I quickly recovered the line, and instructed the men to keep following the fish, as I considered the line was too light, and had already been more heavily strained than I cared for. For the next couple of minutes our fish was quiet, and the men were glad of an easy [spell].

It was not for long though, for after a vicious tug or two away he dashed again for the south bank diagonally down-stream. I let him go, and the boat followed for some fifty yards. Then, right about turn, without a pause, he made for the opposite bank, and on nearing same he rested.

'We ought to have him now, boys,' I said, and instructed them to get the boat beside him. This they did, and for the next few minutes it seemed as if our fish was finished. Neither of the men had yet seen him, and they were wildly excited, and naturally felt elated that all their hard work and the skill it entailed would be rewarded. They could hardly believe that I had ever seen the fish, and numerous were the queries as to its size.

'Is he forty?' 'He is, and more,' was all I would answer. But could I be wrong? 'Well, we have not got him yet, but you ought to be able to see him in a minute or two yourselves.' Some minutes passed. The fish was very quiet, and I was doing my best to lift him. A couple of times I just got a view of the knot on the trace, but each time down it went again.

'Try and bring him closer,' said Bill, 'and I might be able to get him deep with a gaff.' I agreed to this, but warned him not to attempt to gaff him until he got a proper chance of doing so. Bringing the point of my rod round, the fish came with it, and next moment we all got a view.

Bill made a drive and missed, and the next minute our fish was tearing out the line for mid-stream, and apparently fresh, though swimming very near the surface. I had to let him go, and before we got a move on the boat he was sixty or seventy yards away, and again going down-steam. I felt we had lost him, and so did the men.

Bill was down-hearted. I, fortunately, suppressed some forcible language. We soon came up with our fish, and for the first time he showed us his side as he broke the surface of the water. 'If you could bring him back to the bank, sir, you have him,' and slowly we managed to do it.

Bill got the gaff, and, after a minute or so, got his opportunity, and with some difficulty lifted our fish into the boat. A wild yell and hurrah from John greeted his effort. I must own my amazement at the size of the fish on seeing him come into the boat. From the time the men saw him we had put him down as something over forty, but now we wondered if he might be near fifty. Both men were wild with delight, and as proud as blazes of the prowess displayed in the killing.

I had an ouncel in the bag, and as I produced it I must own I felt nervous it would disappoint us. Its maximum was 50lb, and no words I can think of will find expression for our delight when we found that our fish brought the indicator with a flop to the 50lb limit. They immediately wanted to be off to the village to get his full weight and to "wet him" and also anxious, no doubt, to broadcast the news to the numerous cronies who assemble every morning to hear the results of the various catches on the several fisheries.

I, however, demurred. The fish at most I judged from the scale to be a pound or two over the fifty, and since my favourite hole at the top of our water was still untried, I held that the quicker we got there the quicker we would have another. It was only half-past seven, and conditions appeared perfect, after the downpour, for further sport.

[The author proceeded to fish – only to lose the next fish. However he landed a second fish after his boatmen implored him 'not to play it too hard'.]

It was now after eight o'clock, and with both men anxious to show of their catch, I reluctantly agreed to retire for the morrow. We packed up our kit, they shouldered the fish, and I made for my car, which was half a mile down stream, while the men went up the river for the village, where I agreed to meet them later and get the weight and measurements.

On my way down I met the boatman of the water below us, who, of course, inquired if I had any luck. They had seen me arrive and had caught nothing themselves, though out all day. I casually remarked I had got a couple.

Old Frank as casually remarked I had the Devil's own luck, with which I agreed, and on asking the weights of the fish, I told them that one was a beautiful fish of 25–30lb, while the other was fifty or more.

Both looked at me hard, and old Frank, feeling sure I was pulling his leg, turned laughingly away, remarking, 'I know you mean five.'

I left it at that, and made for the car.

Needless to say when I arrived at the village I was told our fish was 51 and a bit. There were drinks galore, and toasts all round, and old Frank, appearing just as I was leaving, late for everything, was very perturbed he had missed the fun. For nine times out of ten he would pass his own door, to find out the day's catch before getting his supper. That evening, however, having met me, though his daughter had told him as he got to his door, that somebody had got a big fish, he promptly denied it as only a tale, and for half an hour after would not believe it.

For fifty odd years he had fished the river, week in and week out, season after season, yet never in that time had he seen a 50-pounder in his boat. He warmly caught hold of my hand to congratulate me and spluttered, 'You have the Devil's own luck.'

MAJOR WALLACE'S 52lb VEFSEN RIVER SALMON
Vol. 1 No. 237

Major Wallace's fish from Norway's Vefsen river was recorded in the first volume of *Giant Salmon* (No. 237). Only the bare facts were documented, taken from *Where to Fish* (1937). However, in March 2009 I came across some more information in a most unlikely place – Major Kenneth Dawson's *Casts From a Salmon Reel* (Herbert Jenkins, 1948), which is a book about salmon fishing in Devonshire!

While practically all the very big salmon of forty pounds and over are males, there is at least one authentic record of a female which reached the quite abnormal weight for her sex of fifty-two pounds.

This nobly-proportioned matron was caught by Major C.W. Wallace, in the Vefsen, a Norwegian river. In other ways, too, she was an interesting dame, who had reached far beyond the allotted span of most salmon. She had evidently been a backward child, for she spent four years in the river before migrating, and then three years in the sea, so that when she first spawned she was a veteran indeed. Not content with breaking records in this way, she made a good recovery, went back to the sea for a year, and then had some more children when aged ten, an age quite equal to that of centenarian in human beings. Still the old lady was irrepressible; again she returned to salt water, lived well for another year, and would again have obeyed Nature's law to increase and multiply, at the colossal age for a salmon of twelve years, if fate in the shape of an angler's lure had not intervened.

I daresay that Major Dawson picked up the details of this salmon's spawning runs from a report in one of the sporting journals (which I have yet to find), in an age when scale-reading had become fashionable. Was the fish caught on a fly or was it caught on bait? Alas, we do not know.

R.G. DEVEREUX'S 52½lb RIVER WYE SALMON
Vol. 1 No. 246

In December 2007, after the publication of *Giant Salmon*, I received some correspondence regarding the Hon. R.G. Devereux and his big Wye salmon (No. 246). Alfred Pope of Bristol informed me that when Dr Stephen Marsh-Smith gave a presentation to the Wye Salmon Fishery Owners Association, he showed a photograph of Devereux with his fish and his gillie, standing in front of their treasured fishing lodge. Ten months later, I received a copy of the photograph from Mr Pope, together with the following note:

> It has taken me nearly a year to locate an image of the 52½lb fish caught by the Hon. R.G. Devereux (No. 246 in your book). Most of the lodge burnt down some 25 years ago. However, our present lodge is very similar in style with the covered walkway and central path as in the photograph.

Although most of the recorded Wye-caught giant salmon were taken on bait of one sort or another, Philip Parkinson, sometime owner of the famous tackle company Sportsfish, who, like Alfred Pope, is a shareholder in the Nyth fishery, pointed out that Devereux appears to have lots of salmon flies in his cap. He also seems to be holding a fly rod that looks to me like a greenheart, so I think we can safely assume that the fish was caught on fly – probably something like one of the big singles on display in the rod room. (This means that Devereux's salmon moves from list 2 to list 1.)

After taking a close look at the facial expressions of Devereux and his gillie, Malcolm Nicholson, it seems to me that they are showing signs of being quite pleased at having caught such a large fish. Accordingly, they represent a transition between Colonel Dalrymple Hamilton's attitude, i.e. looking positively miserable (page 108 of first edition), and the up-to-date Mollie Fitzgerald's expression of sheer pleasure (page 69).

MRS RADCLYFFE'S 53½lb NAMSEN RIVER SALMON
Vol. 1 No. 260

In *Fishing* (1904), *Country Life's* first volume in their Library of Sport, Captain C.E. Radclyffe documents four Norwegian salmon which exceeded the magic weight of 50lb:

> The capture of a 40, or even an occasional 50 pounder is no rare occurrence on the Namsen. Amongst the most notable captures of big fish on this river in recent years, and for which the writer can vouch the weights are correctly given, are the four following: One fish of 58 lbs killed at Vibstad in 1902 by a boatman. A fish of 54 lbs in 1902 by Mr A. Park at Selloeg, and another of 53½lbs caught on the same beat in 1901 by Mrs E. Radclyffe. Also a fish of 53½ lbs by Miss E. Spiller in 1903 at Grande.

Having found a reference in *Where to Fish* to Mrs E. Radclyffe's 53½-pounder, I had in fact included her catch in the first edition of *Giant Salmon* (No. 260), but had no material with which to make an entry in the main text of the book. Was Mrs E. Radclyffe Captain Radclyffe's wife? If so, it is quite likely that she caught her fish on a fly because her husband favoured fly fishing. His note on the choice of flies to use on this river was as follows.

> The subject of flies is always a large and difficult one to tackle, but, to put it briefly, at the beginning of the season and in heavy water, sizes of 6/0 and 5/0 will be found the best. When the water gets clear, and the grilse begin to run, the bag will be greater if sizes of 2/0 and smaller are used. Speaking from personal experience, I have no hesitation in placing the Dusty Miller as *facile princeps*, and next to it the Black Doctor, Jock Scott, and Popham; whilst for casting early in the season, the Grey Eagle and Yellow Eagle are often deadly in this slow stream.

Captain Radclyffe's compelling expression 'for which the writer can vouch' means that the 58lb fish that was killed at Vibstad in 1902 by a boatman is acceptable.

A Norwegian fishing house – a farmhouse that is rented to fishing tenants and their guests during the fishing season.

—AN ENGLISH LADY AND HER DAY'S BAG.

Captain Radclyffe fails to identify the lady in this photograph, although he gave the catch details for two ladies who both succeeded in catching 53½-pounders – Mrs E. Radclyffe and Miss E. Spiller.

E.M. CORBETT'S
54lb EVANGER RIVER SALMON
Vol. 1 No. 263

Although E.M. Corbett's 54-pounder was listed in the first volume of *Giant Salmon* (No. 263), there was no catch account or photograph of the fish. In April 2009 my friend David Beazley, librarian of the Flyfishers' Club, handed me a copy of W.L. Calderwood's book *Salmon* (Edward Arnold, 1938) and pointed out that in it, opposite page 60, is a fine photograph of Corbett with his Evanger fish. The catch details on the information board, pinned to the post above the fish, confirm the catch data – date, weight, length and girth as recorded in my original entry.

There is, unfortunately, no mention of the method used. Corbett also caught a 58lb 6oz salmon on the Vosso River (Vol. 1 No. 311).

E.M. Corbett and his 54-pounder.

JACK NESS'S
54lb RIVER TAY SALMON
Vol. 1 No. 265

On 7 July 2008, some 8 months after the publication of the first volume of *Giant Salmon*, I received a letter from Robert Rattray of Blairgowrie in Perthshire, enclosing two photographs. Each one was of a large salmon, both of which, I thought, would assuredly warrant inclusion if I could find out (a) how much they weighed and (b) who caught them. My next move was to seek the help of the editor of *Trout & Salmon* to see if he would publish the photographs and make an appeal to his readers on my behalf. This he kindly did, and the photographs appeared in the September issue of this popular magazine. Almost at once I received a telephone call from Jim Hutchinson, a retired schoolmaster who lives in Luncarty, a village on Tayside.

We both remembered that we had fished together some 20 or so years ago, and I was pleased to tell him that I still possessed some 'Hutchie' salmon flies that he had tied for me. Subsequently, Mr Hutchinson sent me the following note:

> With regard to the two photographs printed in this month's *Trout & Salmon*, the one with the girl beside the fish depicts Perth angler Jack Ness's salmon of either 54 or 56 pounds, caught, I think, in 1942. The official records show that it came from the Almondmouth beat at the Tay (as noted in the first edition of your book, No. 265), but there seems to be a possibility that it was actually taken in the Catholes beat, several miles upstream.
>
> With regard to the other photograph, there is a possibility that it was a large salmon (No. 238 in the first edition of your book) taken by another Perth angler, 'Chippy' Miller, from the River Earn. However, I can't be certain about my identification of this latter photograph.

Confirmation of Mr Hutchinson's identification of the first salmon's captor and other important catch details came in a letter sent to the editor of *Trout & Salmon* by Michael Smith on 1 September 2008:

> I have the picture in my luncheon hut on the Tay's Burnmouth/Catholes beat at Stanley.
>
> The fish weighed 54lb and was caught by 'Jock' Ness on fly in the Catholes Stream on the Catholes beat on the 19th August 1942. Local

farmer and angler Jimmy Thom at the Byers farm tailed the fish for Jock. Both are now sadly deceased, but were known by me.

In *Giant Salmon* I have only knowingly recorded bait-caught fish with a minimum weight of 60lb, so I have not included the picture of Chippy Miller's fish. The photograph shows that he was using a spinning rod and a fixed-spool reel.

Jack Ness's deep-bodied cock fish. Although the fish was reported as having been caught at Almondmouth, we now know that it was in fact caught at Catholes – a beat between Upper Scone and Stobhall.

MRS 'SAUCY' WILLIAMS'S 54½lb NAMSEN RIVER SALMON
Vol. 1 No. 270

In March 2009, I received an interesting letter from the Revd Nigel Pearson of Caxton in Cambridge, the great grandson of Lt Col. N.G. Pearson, who purchased the Gartland property on the Namsen in Norway from Lady Guest, following the death of her husband Merthyr Guest. Merthyr famously caught a 64lb salmon on the Gartland beat, and I used a photograph of him and his fish in the first volume of *Giant Salmon* (No. 386) to illustrate the dress style of Victorian gentlemen of means.

Revd Pearson informed me that even today, some 120 years later, the rock in the middle of the beat off which the fish was caught is engraved with a record of the event and is still known as Guest rock. As well as giving me details of two big fish caught on the Gartland beat by his grandfather (see page 88), he was able to shed more light on Mrs Williams's 54½-pounder (No. 270 in the first edition), which also came from Gartland:

The dining-room in the family house at Gartland, with two cased fish mounted on the wall.

It was caught on 18th July 1928. She had married the Rev'd Williams, an Anglican missionary, in 1922 in Foochow, and frequently joined the family in Norway for holidays. The fish was 54¼lb, 52in long, and 29in girth. Her nickname was 'Saucy', and I enclose a copy of the verse written to commemorate the catch.

Saucy's Fish

'Twas on a Wednesday evening,
Not a very pleasant night,
The lamp was lighted, and the room was warm,
When those within were startled by an unexpected sight
And all at once were to the window drawn.

Behold our Saucy's face against it pressed;
'I've got a minnow,' said the smiling one.
But those who knew her guilefulness soon guessed
Something as usual (!) to her luck had come.

And then they saw the prize, too big
For any man to carry up alone!
Isak and Bertil and the fish between!
Oh what a monster lay upon the stone.

Fifty-two inches was his noble length,
And twenty-nine, he measured round the chest!
The weight, which must have taken all her strength,
Beat every record, even Father's best.

From 'forty up to fifty' th' excitement grew apace,
Then 'one, two, three, four' followed, and then a 'half' put on.
So now 'Fifty Pounder' he will take his place
And by Marge, our 'Holy Sister', this wondrous deed was done.

So we'll trust in far-off China
Where she goes for other 'fish'
So difficult, and harder to be won –
All grace and tact and wisdom, all that her heart could wish
May guide her till the setting of the sun.

ANOTHER LOOK AT MISS DAVEY'S 59½lb RECORD WYE SALMON
Vol. 1 No. 318

Miss Davey's record spring fish was duly documented in the first volume of *Giant Salmon* (No. 318). So close was it to the magic weight of 60lb that the question of considering a possible weight loss became an interesting possibility. Indeed, the famous pundit on such matters, J. Arthur Hutton, soon – that is to say on 19 May 1923 – climbed into the ring with the following letter addressed to the editor of the *Fishing Gazette*:

THE RECORD SPRING SALMON – THE PERCENTAGES A FISH LOSES IN WEIGHT AFTER CAPTURE

DEAR MARSTON – As regards your note about Miss Davey's 59½lb salmon, it would be most interesting, as a matter of record, to ascertain whether it is the heaviest spring fish caught with the rod in this country. It is a great pity it was not weighed soon after it was landed, as there is always some loss of weight owing to evaporation, which, I believe, takes place after death in all animals. The loss in salmon is not so very great, or at any rate not in the cool weather in spring, though it may be more in the warmer weather of summer. In this connection, I have records of two salmon caught in the Wye, which may be useful. The weights were taken accurately on a steelyard, and not with a spring balance, so they can be depended on.

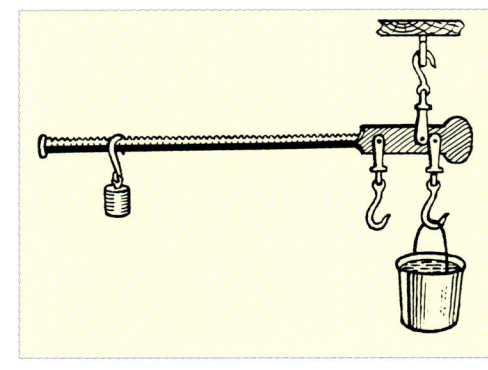

A steelyard

No.1, caught on February 23, at 3.30, weighed 22lb 12oz at 5.00 on the same day. The fish was re-weighed at 1.00 p.m. on February 25, and was then 22lb 7oz. It had therefore lost 5oz, or 1.4 per cent, in 44 hours.

No.2, caught at 1.45 on April 20, weighed 20lb 13oz at 2.00. It was re-weighed as follows:

April 21, 9 a.m., 20lb 9½oz – loss 3½oz (1.05 per cent) in 21 hours
April 21, 6 p.m., 20lb 8½oz – loss 4½oz (1.35 per cent) in 36 hours
April 22, 8 a.m., 20lb 7½oz – loss 5½oz (1.65 per cent) in 50 hours

Apparently, the loss in spring is approximately as follows:
1 per cent in the first 24 hours
¼ per cent in the next 12 hours
¼ per cent in the next 12 hours
or 1½ per cent in 48 hours

As Miss Davey's fish was not weighed until 15 hours after it was caught, I think it is quite safe to assume that it had lost 1 per cent in weight, and therefore, if this is correct, it would have weighed just over 60lb when it was landed.

Yours sincerely
A. HUTTON

Mr Hutton's figures are very interesting. The question of the loss of weight in fish after they have been killed has often been raised but I think Mr Hutton is the first to make actual experiments to test the matter. (ED)

Hutton's conjecture about the weight brought a response from Miss Davey's father, which was published in the *Fishing Gazette* on 26 May 1923.

THE 59½LB RECORD WYE SALMON

DEAR MR MARSTON – I see it is suggested in your issue of May 5 that the big salmon which my daughter caught was not weighed until the next day; this is not so. It was weighed soon after being caught, but under somewhat difficult conditions. It was pitch dark and Mr Barrett had got his spring balance from his fishing hut; he and I supported in our hands the spring balance with the fish suspended, while my daughter held a piece of candle for a light and watched that the salmon's tail was not resting on the ground, and Charley Donald, Mr Merton's gillie, read the scale, making it 59½lb. It was rough and ready and the best we could do at the time; it was weighed properly the next day in Hereford, 17 hours after, and was within a few ounces of what we made it that night in the dark.

I had a steelyard in my hut, which was good for 55lb, and we tried that first, but the fish, of course, took it down with a bump! I am sorry my daughter cannot call it 60lb, but it looks more honest at 59½lb, which is the weight we will always believe it was.

Yours truly

GEORGE DAVEY
Kinnersley Castle,
Kinnersley, Eardisley,
Herefordshire

Another witness then popped up, and the *Fishing Gazette* published his letter on 2 June 1923.

THE RECORD WYE SALMON AND OTHER RECORDS

DEAR MARSTON – In the interest of accuracy I feel I must tell you that Miss Davey's 59½lb salmon was weighed within a few minutes of gaffing, and on my 'Salter' spring balance, which goes up to 60lb. My friends on the Wye often laughed at me for carrying such a big scale, but I said it would come in useful one day, and it did – on March 13 last, with only ½lb to spare! I had the pleasure of seeing the fish hooked and killed, though I was busy elsewhere in the interval killing a 'tiddler' of 19lb – my third that day. Miss Davey's was indeed a wonderful fish, and will, I hope, prove to be the record rod-killed spring fish for this country.

With kind regards,
yours sincerely,

WALTER H. BARRETT
Weymouth

From the above correspondence, it is evident that there was no 'drying out' element to be added to the original weight of Miss Davey's salmon. Instead, we have an endorsement of a claimed weight that some might think was aching for what is nowadays cynically called 'massaging'.

GEORGINA'S BATTLE
Vol. 1 No. 388

In the first volume of *Giant Salmon* (No. 388), I recounted my visit in 1978 to Victoria Cottage, home of the late Georgina Ballantine, as well as to the home of A.P. Lyle, owner of the Glendelvine beat on the River Tay, where Miss Ballantine caught her 64lb fish. The cased fish was mounted on a wall in Mr Lyle's billiard room.

As I have said repeatedly in my books, being able to bring interesting facts to the notice of my readers is utterly dependent on the kindness of the people in possession of such facts responding to my appeals and in many instances sending material to me out of the blue. Such was the case when in June 2009 I received a copy of an account written by Georgina in 1928, at the request of the Laird, A.P. Lyle, some 6 years after the capture of her record fish.

Just a few copies of her account were distributed privately, and fortunately Mark Simmons of Perth Museum and Art Gallery was able to send a draft of the account to me. I take off my hat to Mr Simmons for being so helpful (not for the first time), and merely requiring a copy of the finished piece for museum's records in return.

The scene was set with Georgina's father's urgent command. 'Are you there? Hurry up, you will have to fill a vacancy today; there is a message from Glendelvine to say that the Laird won't be down.'

LANDING OF THE RECORD TAY SALMON

Feverishly the household duties were performed that morning, and as I raced up the river bank to join the boat, how I blessed the Laird for having a headache!

A whole day's fishing, a glorious sunny, autumn day, how I rejoiced to be alive. But such feelings only an angler can understand. To some, the uncertainty of fishing constitutes its chief attraction: to others, the fascination lies in the solitude of the surroundings, the fragrance and beauty of the woods, the songs of the birds, and the enchantment of running water.

And what of the boatmen? One thing is certain, that a good deal of the angler's success or failure depends on the efficiency of the men at the oars. The oarsman that day was one of the finest anglers who ever cast a salmon line on the waters of the mighty Tay – my father – but who, alas, will cast no more.

At tea-time we returned home with three salmon, and as the clock would go back one hour that night, and fishing days were nearing an end,

Miss G.W. Ballantine and her 64lb British record rod-caught salmon. Fixed to the rod is a rarity, a 'Sun and Planet' reel. This photograph was taken by The Raeburn Studio in Perth.

we decided to continue till dusk. Melvin [the second oarsman] knocked off, father and I refreshed ourselves with tea, and leisurely towed the boat to the top of the Boat Pool, a favourite haunt, where the stream is rapid and the current broken.

As is customary when harling, two rods were used, the fly "Wilkinson" on the right, and the dace which I plyed on left. We swung out as the October sun hung low over Birnam Hill, and a few turns at the top brought no result. As the last rays of the great crimson ball shone direct in the eyes of the fish there came a draw upon the line which I was plying, a sharp strike, and connection was established. Then began a Homeric battle. He was hooked well out in the stream above the Bargie Stone, and after a few seconds of very ordinary play, we decided to land him at the broken bank, behind Bargie, on the Murthly side, the slack water there being an advantage. But the fish's plan and ours did not coincide. Whir-r-r! An alarming amount of the line was torn off, the reel screeched as it had never screeched before, the fish careered madly down-stream, leaving only a whirl of spray in its train. Within the fraction of a second the boat was turned down-stream, and down, following hard on the heels of the fish, we were compelled to go. After this first furious rush – about 500 yards – he lost his bearings, and came to a sudden halt close to the north bank, and about 100 yards above the bridge. By that time, however, I had retrieved all the slack line, and had him well under hand, though my arm ached desperately and my left forefinger was cut in an effort to check the line. Here we were in the act of landing, when the fish rolled in to the end of the boat thus offering an opportunity for gaffing. Had a third party been on hand to hold the boat the fish undoubtedly would have been gaffed in the space of ten minutes.

Without delay he righted himself, and sailed off majestically into the deep, ever after that showing a marked disinclination to come to close to quarters. He again elected to go down-stream, and ran out in a line with the North Pier of the bridge. A moment of frightful anxiety followed when he threatened to go through between the piers. But he chose to favour us, and the bridge was safely negotiated. We were now out of the boat, and following the fish, he, meanwhile, keeping about twenty yards from the bank, but showing a tendency to get further out into the current.

Twilight was fading fast, so father thought it wise to run back and fetch the boat, while I hung on to the "refractory beast", who kept advancing and retiring at intervals, but inclining always down-stream. Again boarding the boat we endeavoured to get round to his other side, but that seemed only to spur him on to further effort, and though we worked with him for fully half an hour in mid-stream, he showed no signs of weariness. Then he settled down to intervals of sulking, giving an occasional dive and shake of his head. This period was a steady solid fight for victory between man and monster.

I suggested pelting him with the stones in the boat, but got short cuttings – 'Na, na, we'll try nane o' thae capers'! Eventually we manoeuvred him to the opposite side, where, in the darkness, the trees of the island stood silhouetted against the sky, and where it now seemed as if we were destined to spend the night. Tiring of sulking, the fish began to jag, each jag running like and electric shock down my spine. What language can describe the phases we passed through in that hour; apprehension, hope, and deadly fear. Would the line hold? Was the cast frayed? Was the fish lightly hooked? Would the rod top straighten out if a heavier strain was put on?

Unspoken thoughts such as these passed through our minds. Victory – or failure – was at hand, the next few minutes would see us the happiest or most miserable of human beings. Though utterly exhausted, sheer determination kept me from giving up the rod, as tighter and tighter still came the order, and nearer and nearer came our quarry. By changing my seat to the bow of the boat, and keeping the rod in an upright position, father was enabled to feel with the gaff the knott at the junction of line and cast. Gauging the distance by the length of the cast (3¾ yards), the stroke was delivered, and a wriggling monster was heaved over the seat into the floor of the boat, vigorously flapping his tail.

Again, what eloquence could do justice to such a moment in one's life? Better left to be imagined. He was hooked half a mile further up the river at 6.15; it was now 8.20: two hours and five minutes of nerve-racking anxiety, thrilling excitement, and good stiff work. One thing was decidedly in our favour, we were mercifully ignorant of the size of the fish. From start to finish he never showed himself above the surface. That he was hefty we could well judge from his weight and movements, but nothing more than 35–40 lb was anticipated. He proved to be the heaviest fish of the season, the fish of many seasons, the record for the British Isles.

As we had no spring balance capable of coping with the fish's weight, two passers-by were hailed to carry the "beast", sling on a pole, to Boatlands Farm, where, in the presence of a number of people, it was carefully weighed on a tested steel-yard, half an hour after capture. Though slightly copper-coloured, the fish was in good condition and fresh run, as sea lice were found still adhering to its tail.

It was gifted to Perth Royal Infirmary by Mr Lyle, where it was relished by both patients and staff. A cast was made by P.D. Mallochs, and now the fish displays its lordly proportions at the Mansion House of Glendelvine, where it is looked upon as one of the sporting treasures. An expert's reading of the scales showed that the salmon had not spawned previously, had spent two years in fresh water as a parr, three years in the sea, and would have been six years old in 1923. Arthur Hutton, the celebrated author of *Life History of the Salmon*, mentions in his volume that the condition-factor of this fish works out at 40.6.

Details and Measurements

Captured in Boat Pool, Glendelvine Water, 7.10.22

Size of river	3 feet on bridge gauge
Male fish	64 lbs
Length	54 inches
Girth	28½ inches
Head	12 inches
Tail	11 inches

Day catch – 64, 25, 21, 17 total 127lbs

G.W. Ballantine

A Few Reflections in 2009

Jess Miller, who wrote *The Dunkeld Collection* (1987), an excellent book for all collectors of Hardy reels and baits, informed me (via David Hatwell) that Sir Gavin Lyle, now owner of the original cast of Georgina Ballantine's fish (which was made by Malloch's of Perth), gave him permission in the early 1970s to make twelve fibre-glass reproductions – one of which is on show in Perth Museum and Art Gallery.

Jess Miller commissioned George Jamieson of Edinburgh to make and hand paint all the reproductions, which now have a high market value. Miller also told me that the reel fitted to Miss Ballantine's rod, i.e. the one that is shown in the formal studio photograph, is a rare Malloch's 'Sun and Planet' reel. So far as I am aware, this interesting

In 1978, I took this photograph of Miss Ballantine's home, Victoria Cottage, where she lived with her parents. Her father, who handled the boat while she played the fish, was fisherman for A.P. Lyle.

detail of Georgina's tackle, identified by its bulbous faceted handle and German nickel silver rim, has not previously been noticed.

By some extraordinary coincidence I own a number of letters written by Miss Ballantine to the angling writer Norman Weatherall, who was an informative contributor to angling magazines during the late 1940s, '50s and '60s. However, it was not until May 2009 that I realized the significance of these letters, after David Hatwell drew my attention to the potential interest that salmon fishermen might have in them.

In the late 1960s, when I was researching for my book *Pike* (1971), I read Norman Weatherall's book *Pike Fishing* (Witherby, 1961) and wrote to him expressing the wish that we could meet to discuss various pike matters. I received a reply from his wife, advising me that he had died but saying I could call and search through his papers to see if could find what I was looking for. After my second visit, Mrs Weatherall suggested that I keep all his notes because I was the only person in the years since he had died who had ever shown the slightest interest in them. Among his papers were four letters and some photographs that he had received from Georgina Ballantine.

During the late sixties, Hugh Falkus – whose book *Sea Trout Fishing* had been published – and I became friends. On 1 April 1979, when Hugh was working on his own book *Salmon Fishing* (1984), I sent him Miss Ballantine's letters and photographs, thinking they would be useful material for his forthcoming book. I suggested the letters might interest him and that there was no hurry for their return.

It was just as well that I was in no hurry, because they were not returned to me for nearly 30 years. In 2007, Chris Newton, who wrote a very fine biography of Hugh Falkus, *A Life on the Edge* (Medlar Press, 2007), having been given the opportunity of reading through Falkus's papers, discovered the original package of letters and returned them to me.

Georgina's first letter, written on 22 May 1941, was sent from Victoria Cottage to Weatherall's home in Gerrards Cross.

> Dear Sir
> I had the enquiry this morning re 64 lbs salmon, and herewith send you the photograph. I still have the negative too, but fear it may not be very sharp after nearly twenty years!

This photograph was produced in the 'The Field' a number of years ago. Should it be of any use for your purpose you are welcome to use it. When your article appears I should be interested and grateful to have a copy of the magazine.

Yours very truly
G.W. Ballantine

The Ballantine letters

Georgina wrote a second letter to Weatherall on 28 May 1941:

> I am obliged by your letter of 26th inst. and enclose negatives of fish. I will be glad to have these back, as you will understand they are rather precious to me. Please yourself about the snaps and also the enlargements, it is kind of you to think about such a thing.
>
> Wishing you well in the R.A.F. and a speedy return to normal life.

A third followed on 10 June 1941.

> Very many thanks for returning the negatives of the fish and also for the excellent ¼ plate enlargement, which you did. It is very distinct, and one of the best I have seen. Again thanking you heartily and wishing you well in the future.

After a five-year break, Weatherall must have opened up the correspondence again – only to discover that Georgina, due to declining health, had given up salmon fishing in 1944. Her last letter is reproduced in her own handwriting – other than her address, which was embossed and therefore reproduced badly.

Jean Paul, who holds the Caputh Church Parish Register, told David Hatwell that Georgina Ballantine's father, beside being a fisherman for A.P. Lyle's Glendelvine Estate, was also the last ferryman before the bridge (see page 319 in *Giant Salmon*) was built. Georgina, as well as being a salmon fisher, loved the game of bowls and worked with a local drama group. Like her father, she was the local Registrar, although her father was also Registrar for the Poor. But the last word goes to Jess Miller. In his youth, when he fished on the Tay at Murthly, he often met Miss Ballantine and took advice from her about the location of fish. This is what he had to say: 'She was a lovely lady with sparkling eyes, and I felt it a privilege to talk with her on occasion.'

21/4/46

Dear Mr Weatherall,

Sorry to be so long in replying to your letter of 14th inst. Pressure of work is the reason for delay. I had some difficulty in finding this photograph, it seems to be the last one in my possession. In it, the fish does not show to advantage — he was much thicker than this makes out. However, if it serves your purpose, good & well, you are welcome to it. How glad I am to learn that you have come through safely, & I hope sound in wind & limb. We folk in Scotland suffered very little, but I have lost many of my best friends.

My mother is still alive, age 92, but alas! I have become a chronic rheumatic subject, & only carry on with great difficulty. I fear my fishing days are over tho' I had 6 salmon in 1944 — the heaviest 25 & smallest 9 lbs. With kind wishes for your health & happiness in the years to come

Yours sincerely
G. W. Ballantine

Georgina Ballantine died on 12 April 1970, and her name is engraved on the family gravestone in Caputh churchyard, a distance of some 500 yards from the church.

THE 70lb SALMON THAT CAUSED PROBLEMS
Vol. 1 No. 392

In his book *Fishing: Salmon and Trout* (1885), part of the Badminton library, H. Cholmondeley-Pennell mentions a 70lb salmon on pages 143–4:

> Salter, in one of his works on angling, refers to the capture of a salmon of seventy pounds in the Thames near Fulham, in the year 1789, 'which was subsequently sold to Mr. Howell, a fishmonger in the Minories, for a shilling a pound.'

Unfortunately, Pennell's inadequate documentation made it difficult to trace the reference. Was he referring to Robert Salter's *The Modern Angler* (two editions) or to T.F. Salter's *The Angler's Guide* (nine editions)? Needless to say, although I possessed a copy of both books I drew a blank. Luckily, I was able to consult my friend David Beazley, librarian of the Flyfishers' Club, who found the original quotation on page 150 in the second edition of T.F. Salter's *The Angler's Guide* (1815):

> Salmon will grow to the weight of 50 pounds, and upwards. One was caught in the River Thames, in the year 1789, that weighed nearly seventy pounds and was sold at Mr. Howell's, the fishmonger, opposite America Square, in the Minories, at one shilling per pound.

Suddenly the penny dropped, when I realized there was a familiar ring to this story; indeed, it is told on pages 321–3 (No. 392) in the first volume of *Giant Salmon*. In that entry, I had taken the liberty of converting the weight from 70lb to 64¼lb, knowing that in the late eighteenth century we still used the Dutch pound in Britain.

My reference to the fish was culled from Pennell's popular work *The Angler Naturalist* published in 1863, some 22 years earlier than his equally favoured book *Fishing: Salmon and Trout*. On closer examination of both Pennell's entries, I have noticed some discrepancies, viz.:

The Angler Naturalist spells the fishmonger's name Howel.
Fishing: Salmon and Trout spells the fishmonger's name Howell.
The Angler Naturalist gives the location of capture as near Laleham.
Fishing: Salmon and Trout gives the location of capture as near Fulham.

(Incidentally, it was the naming of Fulham, where I was born, that had fooled me into thinking that this was a new fish.)

Whereas both of Pennell's books give a weight of 70lb, Salter's gives a weight of 'nearly 70 pounds'. Finally, although in *The Angler Naturalist* Pennell tells us that a Mr Wright confirmed the capture of the fish, Mr Wright is not mentioned in Salter's capture account. Of course, close scrutiny of the other seven editions of Salter's *The Angler's Guide* may confirm Mr Wright's involvement as a witness.

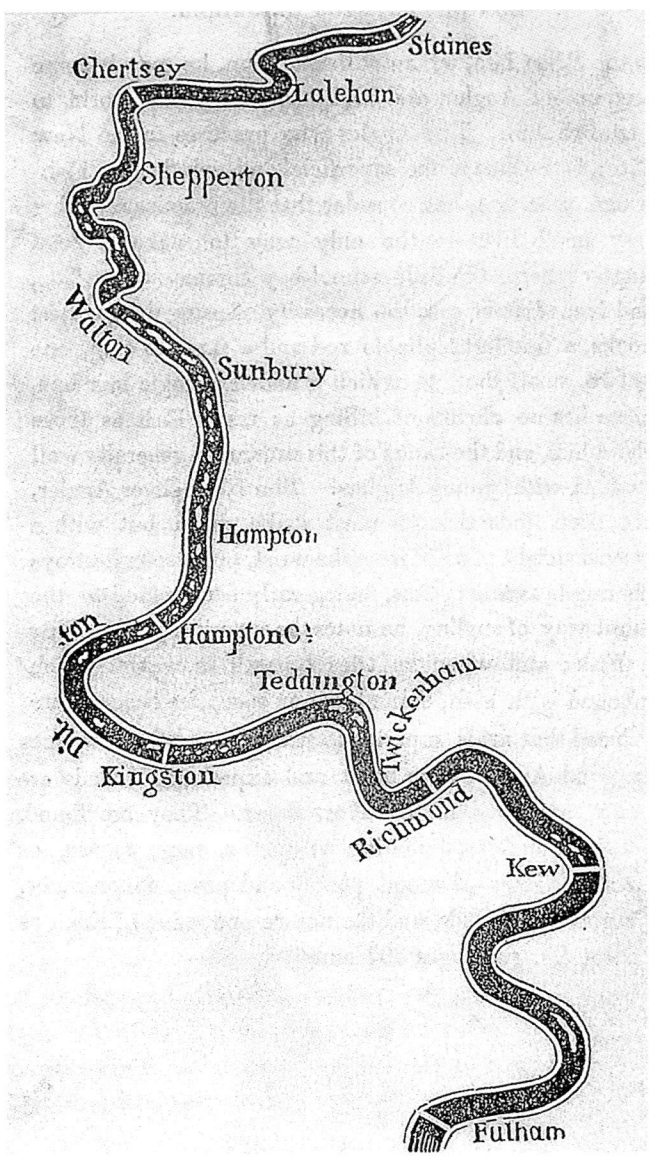

This map of the River Thames, taken from the eighth edition of T.F. Salter's The Angler's Guide *(1833), shows both Laleham and Fulham, and reveals the great distance between the two.*

KAI JACOBSEN'S
68lb 6oz BJØRA SALMON
Vol. 1 No. 414

Kai Jacobsen from København caught this record Bjøra salmon on 28 June 1955. The fish was listed (No. 414) in the first volume of *Giant Salmon* but the photograph, courtesy of *Namsen i Våre Minner*, was not available at the time of publication. Notice the huge girth of this fish – 38in at a guess, doubtless comparable with that of its captor.

AN AMERICAN INSPECTS A BRACE OF TAY GIANTS
Vol. 1 No. 438

Readers of *Giant Salmon* will have noticed that Grove's the fishmonger in London's Bond Street has been frequently mentioned for the habit of displaying exceedingly large salmon as part of an ongoing piscatorial publicity stunt. I dare say that the London fish-market dealers knew that Grove's would pay a high price for any outstanding fish, which were put on public show before being sold on to the shop's hotelier customers.

The *Fishing Gazette* of 29 March 1902 published, on page 232, the following letter from an American visitor to London:

About Large Salmon

DEAR SIR – In the *Fishing Gazette* of March 1 you have some interesting facts regarding large salmon, and I would like to add to them something within my knowledge.

In the spring of 1877 I was in London at Felton's Hotel, St James' Street. I was going next day, it was very early in April, to fish the Galway River, and when the old waiter came to set the table for dinner he informed me that there were two salmon at Grove's, in Bond-Street, which were said to weigh between 70lb and 80lb each. Never having seen a fish approximating this weight, I started at once for Grove's establishment and reached there just as it was being closed for the night. I asked the man in charge if any very large salmon were there, and he said they had received two that morning from the Tay which weighed 67lb and 72lb respectively, that the larger one had been cut as far as the shoulder, but he could show me what remained of him, and all of the smaller one, in the ice box. To this we repaired, and the man very kindly assented to my request that he should weigh in my presence the entire fish. It tipped the scale, as he said it would, at 67lb, and what remained of the other showed me conclusively that the whole of it must have been several pounds heavier, and I was convinced that the man's statement of its weight (72lb) was perfectly credible. The largest salmon I have ever known of being taken with a fly on this side of the Atlantic was caught by Mr Dun on the Grand Cascapedia and weighed

52lb.* I believe that much heavier fish have been taken in nets but have no authentic record of any.

    Yours truly
    D. SAGE
    Albany, New York

When I rediscovered the letter (which had been long filed away) about this brace of Tay giants, my first reaction was that I knew about these fish and that I had already covered the story, so to speak; but on the other hand, I knew nothing of the report of a visiting American's sleuthing activity after he had picked up the gist of the story from a hotel waiter. Then the penny dropped. The same catch data, albeit with different references, appears on page 373 (No. 438) in the first volume of *Giant Salmon*.

    Ultimately, I decided to duplicate the entry simply because the second telling of the story does illuminate the reason why a London fishmonger went out of his way to display exceptionally large salmon to the public. When you think that a waiter in a London hotel managed to excite an American visitor to the extent that he wrote a long letter to the editor of the *Fishing Gazette* and that the editor in turn thought fit to broadcast the information to all his readers, you realize how curious fishermen are about stories of big fish. Moreover, the long-held belief that Americans never write long letters to anyone about anything is seen to be totally false.

    Dean Sage, the author of the letter, later wrote a sumptuous book *The Restigouche and Its Salmon Fishing* (1888), copies of which are extremely scarce and very valuable.

---

*Its actual weight was 54lb. See page 123 (No. 95) in the first volume.

An 1849 watercolour by Scottish artist J.F. Campbell showing salmon fishing boats being poled up the Gilvoniska on the River Alten in Norway.

NOT STRICTLY SPEAKING . . .

DONALD PARRISH'S 51½lb WYE SALMON

One of the privileges of making a rule for my own guidance is that I can break it for a good cause. On page 18 of the first volume of *Giant Salmon*, I set out to describe not only the range but also the limits of my enquiries and subsequent reports on these exceptional fish.

It is important to note that I have *not* explored the catch records of fish between 50lb and 60lb caught on bait, simply because if their numbers were added to the task that I have just completed, the book could not have been published in my lifetime.

Although I can't put Donald Parrish's fish in my lists, because it doesn't fall into one of the categories, I can include it in the book on the basis that it is of particular interest.

In August 1991, Tony Gabba wrote a fine piece for *Trout & Salmon*, entitled 'Tale of an Unsung Salmon', in the course of which he provided what would have been an informative extended caption for a photograph of Parrish's fish.

Donald Parrish's big Wye salmon.

The photograph was taken on the lawn of Brown's Hotel and tearooms in Llandogo and for almost thirty years has hung on the restaurant wall. Generations of salmon fishermen visiting the Bigsweir and Coed-ithel beats of the river have gazed in fascination at the monster fish and wondered at the details of its capture.

As it happens, I was one of the many fishermen who fished at Bigsweir, stayed at Brown's Hotel in Llandogo and gazed in fascination at the photograph of Parrish's whopper.

Parrish caught his fish on a 2½-inch red and gold Devon minnow on Saturday, 26 May 1962. He had hooked it in the Station Pool just below Bigsweir Bridge, and F.E. Swann, the gillie, gaffed it for him when it was played out. Scales were removed for scale reading purposes, revealing that the fish had spent 2 years in the river and 5 years at sea – a year longer than any other Wye 50-pounder.

There is a last little twist to this story, as Tony Gabba pointed out. Donald Parrish continued to fish Bigsweir and continued to use Brown's tearoom, where the framed photograph of the fish hung for nearly 30 years.

Mostly they've remained unaware that Donald Parrish has often been sitting among them, still a member of one of the local syndicates but too modest to announce that he's the man in the photograph, who once caught a 50lb salmon and joined a very exclusive band of fishermen.

HJØRDIS NORDAHL'S
51lb 6oz NAMSEN RIVER SALMON

Although salmon caught on bait are not featured in this book (unless, of course, they exceed 60lb), I have occasionally broken my own rules when the catch is of special interest. In this instance, I would like to draw the reader's attention to the photograph because it is extremely well arranged. (I have an interest in such things, since I was a naval air photographer on H.M.C.S. *The Warrior* in 1946–7.)

The fish, some 48in long, was caught in 1983. It was the biggest Namsen salmon of the year and it took 5 minutes short of an hour to land. How was it caught? On a Rapala of course!

To start with, the fish is perfectly proportioned and in splendid early summer condition. It is hanging full-sided and fills the left-hand side of the frame while the captor, half kneeling and half sitting, fills the right-hand side of the frame. The tree, clouds and rocks combine to fill in the empty spaces most attractively.

TONY COOPER'S
50lb-PLUS ALTEN RIVER SALMON

The following report about a big fish from the Alten river (usually known as the Alta these days) was given to my friend Dr Roy Flury by Tony Cooper himself.

On the afternoon of 17 July 2001, I was fishing the Harestrommen pool on the Sautso stretch of the Alta. The boatmen, who both played a vital role in the proceedings, were Svein Ole Arnesen and Svein Lyon Holten, and I was fishing with a 15 foot rod, a floating line and a 25lb leader. The tube fly was a 1½ inch Willie Gunn. About a quarter of the way down the fast-flowing pool I had a strong take and the fish soon showed it meant business with a series of spectacular jumps. We followed the fish in the boat, keeping the pressure on, and after 20 minutes I was able to clamber out on to the shingle beach and play the fish from there. However, it soon became clear that the fish was intent on swimming downstream and I got back into the boat to continue the struggle.

The fish was gradually tiring and having reached a good position below it, I was on the bank again and slowly brought it round to Ole Arnesen who was holding the huge Alta net. This first attempt to net it ended up with much shouting from the fishermen and tail slapping from the fish, mainly because it appeared to be too big for the frame of the net. Away it went back to the middle of the river but, fortunately, it was well hooked and I was able to swing it around with the help of the current and slowly bring its head over the net for the second time. It was then 'bundled'

On his return to England, Tony Cooper – who works with Frontiers in Gloucestershire – commissioned this model of his big fish, superbly carved by Roger Brookes of Kingsland.

in and safely landed. Some forty minutes had elapsed since the take.

It was a handsome cock fish, in very good condition, and measured just over 53 inches in length and 30 inches in girth. The scales hit the 50lb mark but that was their limit. The fish was given a farewell kiss, returned to the water and held in the current to recover before being released. The fish was known to be over 50lb, but by how much? After some discussion the experienced boatmen estimated the weight at 26 kilos, just over 57lb.

DONAL C. O'BRIEN'S 52lb GRAND CASCAPEDIA SALMON

In October 2008, Donal O'Brien, from New Canaan in Connecticut, wrote to tell me how much he had enjoyed The Domesday Book of Giant Salmon, and to provide details of his own best catch. Mr O'Brien has long been an ardent Atlantic salmon fisherman, and in his letter he noted:

> I am the oldest serving acting director of the Atlantic Salmon Federation (US). I am 75, and I have been fishing for Atlantic salmon ever since I married my wife, Katharine, in 1956. I took a 47lb salmon in 1982 and in 2004 I caught and released a salmon that, with careful measurements, was estimated at 52lb. Both fish were taken on the Grand Cascapedia, which, not surprisingly, is my favorite river.

What follows has been culled from Donal O'Brien's fishing log and clearly describes the experiences of Donal and his wife Katie in taking the bigger fish.

Date	Location	Pool	Weather
Saturday, 31 July 2004	Camp Tracadie, Grand Cascapedia, Gaspe, Quebec, Canada	Three Islands Home Pool	Light rain, overcast in a.m., perfect conditions; thick mist and fog, heavy rain in p.m.

This model of Donal O'Brien's fish was carved by Stephen Smith of Jamestown.

In the afternoon we left camp at 5.00 p.m. for our last evening of fishing. Decided to start in Lower Lost Channel, which had not been fished all day. Started at the lip, then fished from the culvert down to the rock. All our drops fished well, especially the lip – the fly was fishing naturally, at exactly the right level, just below the slick surface. It was raining lightly, with mist coming off of the water, when we went into the pool. It would soon be a steady, heavy rain and the mist would turn into a swirling fog. We never had a rise. Saw one jumping fish, off the rock.

Rain was really coming down hard as we headed for Three Islands. Arrived just before 7.00 p.m. Shawn [Harrison, the O'Briens' guide] took us way up the camp side of the river – almost to Beaver Run, which is the long flat pool above Three Islands Run. We had never fished this high up. There was a small pocket of reasonably deep water with rapids on either side. This was where Shawn wanted us to fish. I was doubtful.

'Have you ever taken a fish this high up?'

'Oh, yes,' said Shawn, 'more than a couple, quite a few.'

I had on a #6 low water, single hook, green stonefly and was fishing a singled-handed 10ft Loomis with a 12lb tippet and a 9 weight line on a Bogdan 100.

I started with enough line to clear the first rapids – maybe 25ft – and five casts later a fish took the fly. I said, 'I don't think it's very big.' Then he began to move out of the pool, and I knew immediately that I was wrong. I had a big fish, a very big one. He was soon in the deep water at the bottom of the run, holding deep, moving very slowly, head pounding, line throbbing as he methodically headed up river. And then he made his first run, diagonally across the river, ending in a surface-breaking 'thrash', which was not a jump but enough for us to see he was a great fish. I brought him back into the heart of the pool. More head pounding, very deep, followed, and another run toward the end of the pool, this one well into the backing. Again, I brought him back in. We had now moved down river and I was fighting the fish by the salmon pen, where they keep the fish for their milt and roe. I was about 10 yards up from the Three Islands boat landing, with deep, relatively still water in front of me, an excellent place to fight a big fish. There were more runs diagonally across river, from which I kept bringing him back into the pool, more holding in the center of the pool, and then more of the same – runs, not as long, head pounding, holding deep, line throbbing, rain heavy and steady, and suddenly I had him up on top and I was leading him, 'swimming' him, toward the shore.

Normally – in fact always – I ask my guide simply to hold the net and I try to 'drop' the salmon into it. Shawn was right at my side where I wanted him, but I had a hunch and I acted on it. We were now just a few yards from the landing. It was very dark. Heavy rain and swirling fog at the end of the day made visibility very poor. The salmon was high in the water and I was 'swimming' him with ease. I made a decision. I said, 'Shawn, take him.'

Shawn, moving quickly with his long legs, was at the fish in a flash, placing the net under his head and lifting him up. The salmon never knew what had hit him. He could not have been on for much more than half an hour. Shawn brought him to us and we could not believe what was in the net. He was absolutely huge.

The first thing, which struck all of us, was his width – his thickness – from the tip of his nose right down to his tail, and his depth. One could walk down his back. He looked exactly like a small bluefin tuna – that was his shape. He was the largest salmon I had ever seen in a lifetime of fishing, and I said, in a second, 'He is larger than my 47-pounder,' which I had taken on June 16, 1982 in Mrs Guest's pool in the Engelhard water. The 47lb salmon was a female, but long and not that thick. She had good depth but thinned out from above the anal fin down to the tail. I have a fiberglass mount of this fish, and I look at her every day. I know her size backward and forward. The salmon I had just taken was bigger and I said so again. In fact, with a pause, and not without a little hesitation, I said, 'He is 50lb.'

I always carry a waterproof tape measure, and we did our best to get his measurements for the formula. He was 'green' and anything but calm and cooperative, but we made every effort to be accurate. We measured his length at an easy 48 inches. I believe he was actually longer, since he was not stretched out flat, as is the case when dead fish are measured. Measured dead, I am sure he would have been 49 inches. However, it was his depth and width – his girth – that gave him his great size. We had some trouble getting this measurement since the tape slipped forward from the high point of his dorsal fin, where he was thickest. Nevertheless, below the dorsal, the tape showed a full 28 inches. Shawn said, 'Call it 29 inches,' and then, '30 inches.' This is how we would leave it.

We were right by the live fish pen and we briefly thought of putting him in it, but it took only seconds to decide that I did not want to do this. I did not want him handled, and milked, and possibly killed. I wanted him back in the river. Shawn lifted him once again. He was absolutely perfect. He was so thick and deep that his head was not out of proportion with his body, which is often the case with large males. He was not fresh, but there was no large hook bill. He was the most beautifully proportioned salmon of any size I have ever seen. Shawn moved him into the deeper water, held him in the current and then let him go. With a sweep of his huge tail, he was off in a flash. He did not swim away, he exploded away. I think he had barely known that he was hooked. In truth, we stole him on that first pass as I 'swam' him toward shore, coming easy, in the heavy rain and darkness. He never knew that Shawn was near him until he was in the net. It was about a quarter to eight when we let him go.

Back at camp, Katie took out her calculator and we applied the formula: girth times girth times length divided by 800 equals weight. We started with a girth of 30 inches: 30 x 30 x 48 ÷ 800 = 54lb. We then tried the formula with a 29 inch girth – a measurement in which we had great confidence. It came out to 50½lb. I do not think anyone was very surprised by these results. We would later make various other estimates based on slight modifications of girth and length.

The Three Islands salmon looked like an entirely different species from the 1982 fish from Mrs Guest's pool. The 1982 fish was long and lanky. She seemed dwarfed by the 2004 fish. If the 1982 fish was shaped like a torpedo, the 2004 fish was shaped like a depth charge.

Some after thoughts: I do not believe Shawn, as able as he is, could have netted the salmon on that first pass if the fish had been hooked and played in daylight. The salmon would surely have seen him. But it was almost dark and the heavy rain was peppering the surface. I also never 'held' the fish. I was simply leading him, 'swimming' him to shore with very little pressure, using only the rod and the drag on the reel. And, although he was close to the surface, he was still quite deep when Shawn took him. If Shawn had missed, that fish would have been off like a rocket. He was so 'green' that it would be hard to predict what the outcome would have been. We were told later that when 'you miss a great fish on the first chance, you have lost your best chance.' They know exactly where the danger lies and will do everything they can to avoid it.

KATRINE OPGÅRD'S 53½lb ALTEN RIVER SALMON

A tremendous run of big fish taken from Norway's Alten River in 2008 included something like nine 50-pounders. One of them, a 53½lb fish, was caught on 17 June by young Katrine Opgård.

From the scant information I received initially, it appeared that the fish was caught on fly. Accordingly, I reserved a place in my lists for Katrine's fish, and sat back to wait for more documentation and a catch account to arrive. In the event it came in a letter from Dr Roy Flury just two days before I planned to hand over the manuscript to the publishers.

The report of Katrine Opgård's fish which was caught in 2008 was kindly sent to me by Ivar Leinan of the Alta Association. He had translated it into English from an article in the *Altenposten*. The fishing season on Alta begins on June 1st. Traditionally, the fishing is reserved for the local people for three weeks until midnight on June 23rd. Special permits are sold for a few days fishing or for the whole three week period. Katrine was one of those lucky locals and at the age of fifteen she set out to catch her first salmon. This was achieved on Thursday, June 12th when she landed a fish of a mere 35lb! Five days later, on June 17th, at the end of an astonishing day, she described her adventures to journalists from the *Altenposten*.

'I was spinning with a spoon from the bank and within ten minutes I was

This photograph of Ms Opgård and her fish, taken by Magne Kveseth, appeared on Salmon Fishing Updates, *an internet site for salmon anglers.*

into a fish. I realised very quickly that this fish was not a kelt. I was not able to control it – it just did what it wanted. I tried to be hard on it as I had already lost two fish earlier in the week and I didn't want that to happen again! Some people who were watching from the bank told me afterwards that they were sure I was going to lose the fish because I was being so hard on it.

In spite of the strong check on my reel, the fish went straight upstream at a crazy speed into the fast water. I understood what was going to happen. When the fish turned downstream it would be gone in a flash. I did not have any waders and I was on the bank with no boat. Luckily, there were some experienced fishermen nearby. They helped me to find a path round some difficult trees. The fish was away again with me chasing after it. I was running and jumping and lost one of my shoes before reaching quieter water 300 metres downriver. Then I was lucky for the second time. It was not only me who had seen it was a big fish for Tormod Opgård suddenly appeared in his boat with two others. They took me into the boat with them and there I stood, with no shoes on, playing a big male salmon. From then on it all went well and we soon landed the fish. Minutes later I had such a shock when I couldn't believe my eyes. As Tormod lifted the fish I saw the spoon was hooked into the tail and worst of all the fish had drowned. I had been so hard with it in the fast current that it could not breathe.'

The fish weighed 53½lb and had taken just over an hour to land. It had been hooked in a pool called Pahtakorva, which is well towards the lower end of the river.

After she had told her story of the catch there was some friendly teasing. Katrine enjoys football and is a loyal Liverpool supporter. It was suggested that she should sell the fish to pay for a trip to Liverpool and see her team play. When another journalist remarked that there was little point as they would certainly lose again if they played Chelsea, she asked for a different reporter.

Although I have removed Katrine's fish from the lists, I am sure readers will understand why her account and photograph remain. In fact, it is very rare to land a salmon of such a size hooked in the tail but, interestingly, it has been done on the Alten before. Mrs Jules Vernes was fishing in much the same part of the river with the Duke of Roxburghe's party in 1965 when she hooked a fish in the ventral fin. The fish weighed 50lb, and is recorded as taking three hours to land!

RAGNOR TENVIK'S 54½lb NAMSEN RIVER SALMON

On 7 June 2009, Ragnor Tenvik of Sanderfjord was fishing with boatman Tor Kjetil Nagellhus. They were harling on what was once Norway's most famous big-fish river, the Namsen. Tenvik knew the beat at Upper Vibstad well, because he had fished it for more than 20 years, during which time his best fish weighed 26½lb. However, on this fateful day, after all other fishermen had gone home, he landed a massive salmon that was more than twice as big – indeed, it was the biggest salmon taken on the Namsen for 25 years.

On 18 July 2009, I received a letter from David Hatwell telling me that Ragnor Tenvik caught his fish on a 6cm Finnish Wobbler bait, which means that I cannot place it on any of the lists that form the backbone of this book, but of course the fish could be regarded as an item of special interest, which it most assuredly is. The fact that it was taken on the Namsen suggests a recovery of this most famous of all Norwegian big-fish rivers, which had been suffering from a most dreadful decline. The scale reading is also of considerable interest, because it demonstrates that the fish spent 3 years in the river before smolting, and three years at sea, growing at a fast rate – the normal lifestyle for a Norwegian 50-pounder.

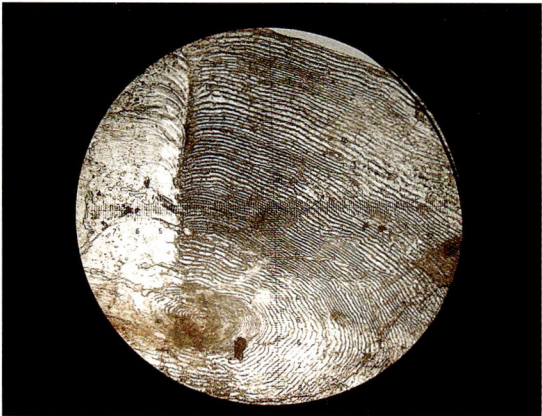

The moon-like image of a scale from Ragnor Tenvik's fish clearly shows the six winters of its life, in the form of annuli or growth checks – the rings indicating growth are closer together during the winter, when growth slows down.

Ragnor Tenvik and his boatman, Tor Kjetil Nagellhus with Ragnor's 54½lb salmon.

APPENDICES

Appendix 1
NETTED MONSTERS FROM THE TAY AND ELSEWHERE

Although it's not every salmon fisherman's cup of tea to read about huge salmon that have been caught in nets, it is nevertheless instructive to some of us to be given details of the size and frequency of huge salmon that, but for the estuary nets, would have made it back to their native streams. For many years, reports of the taking of large salmon were usually investigated by Henry Ffennell. From time to time his watchdog activities were taken up and commented on by other correspondents. One of these, whose nom de plume was Grant, had his letter published in the *Fishing Gazette* on 20 October 1894:

THE LARGEST SALMON OF MODERN TIMES

SIR – In your issue of the 13th inst. Mr. Henry Ffennell writes "Since the capture in 1870 of the Tay salmon of 70lb., which was cast by poor Frank Buckland, attempts have been made from time to time to foist off various bogus particulars of heavier weight, but that fish must still remain the largest salmon of modern times."

I may mention the *Field* of Sept. 1 last, under heading "Net Fishing Season on the Tay, 1894", gives a list of highest weight salmon captured, extending back to the 70lb. fish in 1870 referred to by Mr. Ffennell, and therein for the year 1877 four fish are enumerated weighing 60lb., 61lb., 64lb., and 73lb. respectively – I am, sir, yours, &c.

What is probably the largest recorded catch of 50lb salmon (seven) from one river in a season (1885) was mentioned in a report on the relative productivity of British salmon rivers that was published in the *Fishing Gazette* on 15 February 1890:

A great number of large salmon were captured during 1885, both by net and rod. On the Tay, salmon of 56lb., 55lb., 54lb., 53lb., 52lb., 51½lb., 50lb. and 49lb. were taken by the nets, and a very large number between the last-mentioned weight and 30lb. More than fifty salmon, averaging 45lb. each, are estimated to have been taken during the month of August. The largest fish taken by the rod was captured on the Stobhall water, and weighed

47lb.; but a great number were caught by anglers on various stretches of the river upwards of 30lb. weight.

However the most productive river in 1885 was the Aberdeenshire Dee.

The term "magnificent" applied to the Usk on account of its wonderful yield of fish to the rod is thoroughly appropriate, but its magnificence is entirely dwarfed by that of the Aberdeenshire Dee, if we are to accept as gospel the statement made by the Scotch Fishery Board in their annual report (1886) to the Government, that: "no fewer than six thousand fish are said to have been taken by the rod on the Aberdeenshire Dee during the season of 1885; and when it is considered that at least ten thousand were taken by anglers in the course of the two previous seasons, it may be doubted whether any salmon river in Europe can show a better return."

In 1908, Henry Ffennell had a survey published, entitled *Salmon Fishing* in 1907, a copy of which has kindly been given to me by Mark Cope. The survey started with a summary of the season's largest netted fish:

LARGE NET FISH OF THE YEAR

The number of Salmon of 50lbs., and upwards, taken in the nets during 1907, included some of the finest specimens, but 'monsters' were not so numerous as in former years. The Tay yielded a fine fish of 57½lbs., which I had the opportunity of seeing in Mr. Grove's shop in Bond Street. It measured 4 ft. 5 ½ ins, girth, 2 ft. 4½ins. It was taken on the 24th of May. There were also taken on the Tay one 54lbs., one 52lbs. and 51lbs. In the North and South Esk district one 53lbs. and one 51lbs. On the coast off the Scotch Dee one 52lbs. I heard also that a Salmon of 50lbs. was taken in the Spey district, and that a Salmon of 55½lbs. said to have been taken in the Severn, was shown in a shop at Birmingham.

The second list in his survey dealt with rod-caught fish, and it is interesting to note that the authenticity of the largest fish – 61½lb, No. 345 in the first volume of *Giant Salmon* – is questioned.

Large Rod Fish of the Season

The heaviest rod fish of 1907 was taken in the Tay district, and weighed 61½lbs. It measured 4ft. 6ins. long, and was said to have been an ugly monster. It was one of the largest fish taken from the river since the celebrated 'King of Scots' was weighed and measured in London by Frank Buckland in 1870. That celebrity, as it lay in the shop in Arabella Road, near Victoria Station, weighed just under 70lbs. No doubt when it was first taken out of the water it weighed several pounds more. There was considerable doubt at first as to the way in which the big fish of 1907 was taken. The head was sent to Mr. Mallock [sic] of Perth to set up, and he was under the impression that it had been landed in the nets. At the time of the capture he wrote to say he believed the fish had been caught in the nets. "There were no hook marks in its mouth, and when it was being examined, two small sprats, in fresh condition, were found in its gullet. Sparling boats were in operation a little way down the river, where the fish is alleged to have been caught, and it was while the fish were wriggling in the bag of the net, that the sprats found their way into its gullet." Mr. Thomas Stewart, of Caledonian Road Park, however writes to say that the fish was caught by him fishing with worm. It was taken on the 16th of October in the river, 1½ miles below Perth.

Appendix 2
THAMES SALMON

Although salmon weighing less than 50lb are not the main feature of this book, I believe that the subject of large Thames salmon is of such interest as to warrant a check on the biggest recorded specimens, especially in the knowledge that wild Thames salmon – large or small – no longer exist.

Sir Herbert Maxwell, ever the optimist, set the scene in his *Salmon and Seatrout* (1898) for the reintroduction of the species:

> The Thames remained a prolific salmon river after Walton's day. The last salmon was killed at Boulter's Lock, near Taplow, in 1824, when the race succumbed to the combined efforts of pollution and navigation dams. But the lower reaches of the river now are far purer than the Tyne at Newcastle: twice, within the last three years, I have seen small fish (probably bleak or dace) swimming alongside the terrace of the House of Commons, and probably it requires but a sustained effort to restore the Thames as a salmon river. There are still plenty of eels in it; adult eels must descend to the sea to spawn, and young elvers ascend, otherwise the race had long since been extinct in this river. In order to lure salmon back to this river where they abounded almost in living memory, it would be necessary to conduct artificial propagation of a spirited scale. The conditions as to purity are far more favourable than when last was attempted under the auspices of Mr. Buckland.

J.F. Hampton wrote a piece for *Angling* magazine (July 1942) about Thames salmon, in which he noted details of an extraordinary large catch that was documented in the Church Warden's book for Wandsworth in 1580. He also included a list of the prices that fishermen or fishmongers obtained for their salmon over a period of 334 years.

> 1486 – 6s.8d. paid by Brotherhood of Corpus Christi at Maidstone. This salmon was obtained from Shene, or Sheen (now Richmond)
>
> 1629 – £2 10s. 0d. State Papers paid to Henry Millington
> 1749 – 1s. 0d. per lb
> 1795 – 5s. 0d. per lb
> 1797 – 2s 0d. per lb
> 1806 – £9 18s. 0d. for a 35lb fish

1807 – 7s. 6d. per lb
1820 – £1 1s. 0d. per lb

Just to prove how rare salmon were becoming, Hampton added:

> In 1821 thirty shillings per pound were offered for Thames salmon to be used at the Coronation Banquet of George IV; it was not, however, possible to purchase any even at this high price. The low price in 1749 is accounted for by phenomenal catches: "two of the greatest draughts of salmon were taken in the Thames below Richmond that have been known for some years, one net having 35 salmon in it and the other 22." It was, however, only a flash in the pan, the decline of the fishery had already commenced.
> Between 1794 and 1821, 483 salmon were captured at Boulter's Lock, Maidenhead, averaging 15lb apiece. The end, however, was not far off. Apart from one or two gallant fish, which have been caught within recent years in tidal reaches of the river, the last salmon was taken from the Thames in 1833.

Notice that Hampton says the last Thames salmon was caught in 1833, whereas Maxwell has it that the last salmon was killed in 1824. One or two heavyweight specimens were caught from time to time; the *London Chronicle* of 11 June 1760 records the following:

THE LEA

> On Wednesday last, a salmon that weighed upwards of 32lbs was taken in Hackney River near Brasier's Ferry.

Those details indicate that it was a Thames salmon, probably wandering prior to making a run up its natal stream.
In Edward Hamilton's book *Fly-Fishing – Salmon, Trout & Grayling* (1891), we are told that the Reverend G. Venables reported that in 1780 his father caught upwards of 50 salmon in the reach of the Thames opposite Clevendon Spring.

> Mr Venables' father also records that he caught a salmon in the Buck Pool on the 26th June, 1793, weighing 42lbs., length, 4ft. 1 in.

On page 150 in the second edition of T.F. Salter's *The Angler's Guide* (1815), we read:

> Salmon will grow to the weight of 50 pounds, and upwards. One was

caught in the River Thames, in the year 1789, that weighed nearly seventy pounds and was sold at Mr. Howells, the fishmonger, opposite America Square, in the Minories, at one shilling per pound.

For more details of this fish see Additions No. A24 (The 70lb Salmon that Caused Problems). See also the report of T.R. Sachs quoted in No.77 (The Coxens of Twickenham):

LARGE THAMES SALMON

SIR – In looking over my album of fishing events, I came across the following, which I noted at the time: Richard Coxen, fisherman of Twickenham, and three others, caught a salmon of 72½lb. in 1820, and sold it to Watkins of Bond Street, for 8s. 6d. per lb.

From the above evidence, the Thames in its prime was obviously a big-fish river of the most productive kind.

Appendix 3
MONA'S TABLE AND OTHER WEIGHT/LENGTH TABLES

On 3 May 1902, the *Fishing Gazette* published a list of big salmon put together by that ever helpful and pragmatic contributor Henry Ffennell. Ffennell, is convinced that the possession of such data, although of great interest, would not enable readers to forecast the weight of a salmon by juggling with measurements.

Historically, pundits have always been keen to devise a table that would forecast the weight of a salmon by such means. Ffennell had a different approach – he had an arrangement with the famous fishmonger Messrs Groves of Bond Street that he would be notified of the arrival of every large salmon, so that he could call by to measure and carefully weigh it.

I have arranged Ffennell's list so that the statistics of the nineteen fish mentioned can be consulted at a glance. I dare say that the measurements of three of the fish – numbers 1, 4 and 10 – will catch the reader's eye, because although all three fish have a length of 53in, the weights are 68lb, 58lb and 52lb respectively.

Henry Ffennell's List Rearranged

No	Where Caught	Weight	Length	Girth
1	Tay	68	53	30½
2	Montrose	63	55	29
3	Shannon	60	49	30½
4	Tay	58	53	27
5	Shannon	56	51	29
6	Severn	55	50	30½
7	Shannon	55	50	30½
8	Tay	54½	52	28½
9	Tay	54	51	28
10	Severn	52	53	26½
11	Wye	51	50	27
12	Fifeshire Coast	51	49	29½
13	Severn	50½	52	27
14	Tay	50	50	28
15	Shannon	50	47	29
16	Forth	49½	48	27
17	Shannon	45	46½	28
18	Tay	43½	49	27½
19	Shannon	42½	44	27½

Irish journalist William Fletcher wrote under the nom de plume 'Mona', a name that is synonymous with a table that uses a pike's length to forecast its weight. After it was first published by the *Fishing Gazette* on 28 September 1918, the table was widely quoted during the next 90 years, although its usefulness is diminished by the fact that big pike are all hen fish, and subject to a weight loss of up to 20 per cent immediately after spawning. Furthermore, the pike's ability to swallow dietary items of up to one third of its own weight seriously complicates the issue. Mona's scale is based on the supposition that a pike of 40in – measured from neb to fork – weighs 20lb.

Before he died in May 1919, Mona made a similar table to forecast the weight of salmon, based on the supposition that a salmon of 36in – measured from neb to fork – weighs 20lb. In a note published in the *Fishing Gazette* he added, 'We find the weight of any salmon in pounds to be the cube of its length multiplied by 0.000428; thus a 40in salmon should weigh 27.3lb, one of 45in 39lb, a 50in fish 53.5lb, and so on.'

Since most of the really big salmon (i.e. those over 50lb) are cock fish that are only fished for when their gonads are fully primed,[1] the greater accuracy of the salmon table is understandable.

Mona was a well-educated, widely experienced and gifted writer, who excelled in mathematics, and in his obituary in the *Fishing Gazette* on 7 June 1919, we are told how he came to join the staff of *The Irish Field*. It occurred in this fashion:

> In a weak moment a short article upon that mysteriously constituted fish, the salmon, was accepted. It duly appeared in print. The salmon is an uncanny fish in many respects. Only experts on fish-life dare to write or theorise about its habits. The short article we printed, however, would appear to have contained every possible popular error conceived about salmon, and the result was quite a journalistic storm. He was simply aghast at the crop of errors, which *The Irish Field* expounded solemnly as facts. We were not aware at the time, too, that he was really an authority upon the fish, as far as anyone can be an authority upon salmon. But he wrote so well, so authoritatively, so mildly critical, and with such a fund of real practical knowledge and love of angling, that he was induced to contribute regularly to the paper, and we are glad to say it was to him a labour of love.
>
> How he came to select his nom de plume we never knew. It has associations with the Isle of Man, yet we never heard of him having anything in kin with that island. He used it as far back as when he was sojourning in India, and his own explanation of it was humorous, it standing, he said, for a Man of No Account.

Although Mona was one of the earlier angling writers to propose a formula for converting length into weight, an existing scale already appealed to salmon fishermen who had an arithmetical flair, viz.:

> Length, plus one-third of the Length, multiplied by the square of the Girth, and divided by 100, would give the weight in pounds. Thus a fish 36in long with a girth of 20in should weigh 19.2lb: $\frac{(36+12) \times 400}{100} = 19.2$

> A few inquisitive fishermen noticed variations in the weight of salmon of the same length but caught in different rivers. For example, it was evident that Norwegian salmon from the Vosso River, inch for inch, were heavier than, say, Wye salmon. The outcome was the invention of the famous Sturdy Scale.

Arthur Hutton in *Wye Salmon and Other Fish* (John Sherratt & Son 1949) noticed that Sturdy's Scale was based on data obtained from salmon caught on Sturdy's own beat (the Evanger Beat) on the Vosso River. For more information on the subject, Hutton advises his readers to consult Edward Corbett's excellent paper 'The Length and Weight of Salmon', published in *Trout & Salmon* magazine in September 1922. In essence, Sturdy's formula is: four-thirds (1.3333) times the length of the fish, times the square of its girth, divided by 1000. The table appears in full in the first edition of *Giant Salmon*.

In the second quarter of the twentieth century, all the interest in length/weight issues seemed to activate the pundits, who needed something to be contentious about, with the result that the 'condition factor' of any reported big fish had to be considered. Personally, I believe the term to be misleading because it appears to pre-suppose that an increase in bulk relative to length equals superior condition, which isn't necessarily true. I am reminded of a piece I wrote for an Irish angling magazine many years ago, drawing attention to information on the noticeable difference in the weight/length relationship found in salmon that ran into one particular Irish lough. Small shoals of these fish ran up into the lough during the summer months, after almost every rainstorm. Later in the season, when the water conditions were suitable, these fish then ran into their natal stream (one of two streams) prior to spawning. This is what I wrote:

> By and large, populations of all living creatures that have had time to exploit a particular niche have adapted themselves to their habitat to an extraordinary degree. For example, two readily identifiable varieties of salmon can be caught in Co. Donegal's Lough Eske. One type – long and lean, almost kelt-like in appearance – is adapted to run up the tortuous River Corabber, which falls steeply from the Blue Stack Mountains before it disgorges into the head of Lough Eske, while the other type – thickset, handsome and short – runs the River Loweymore, which meanders through a lowland valley before flowing into the south-west side of the lough. This was first brought to my notice by Sidney Spencer, the author of *Salmon and Sea Trout in Wild Places*. You would never, he told me when I fished with him, catch these widely differentiated forms of the same species in the 'wrong river'[2] and so far as my own catches are concerned I would agree.

From the difference in the appearance of these fish we can be sure that the 'condition factor' for the Corabber fish would not be impressive, but they were – just the same – great fighters.

Edward Corbett's 'condition factor' was based on the fact that 'the weight of cylindrical bodies varies with the cube of the length', while Hutton, on page 122 of his fine book, provides a simplified instruction, which is easy to follow:

> One can easily ascertain the factor of any Salmon of known length (in

inches) and of known weight (in pounds) by multiplying the weight by 100,000 and by dividing by the cube of the length. Here are two examples.

A 10-pound fish, 30in long $30 \times 30 \times 30 = 27,000$
                                     $$\frac{10 \times 100,000}{27,000} = 37$$

A 27-pound fish, 40in long $40 \times 40 \times 40 = 64,000$
                                     $$\frac{27 \times 100,000}{64,000} = 42.2$$

In this way one can compare fish with fish or the Salmon of one river with those of another river. I have known Salmon with factors over 50, but anything over 40 is a very good fish. In order to save a lot of calculating, my advice to my readers is buy, borrow or steal one of Corbett's 'Condition Calculators'.

Hutton demonstrated 20 years of devotion by recording every Wye salmon caught weighing over 50lb. The list was published in the *Fishing Gazette* on 25 March 1939. Notice that Hutton revealed his assiduity, for keeping what he thought were important records, by calculating the condition factor for all eleven fish as well as their age by scale reading – only to find from the latter that every fish was the same age, i.e. six years old. It is interesting to compare Hutton's list (below) with H.A. Gilbert's list in *Large Wye Salmon* (see Appendix 5, page 214).

> Dear Marston – I have just received the scales of a 'portmanteau' from the Wye, caught on March 15 by Professor Merton at Winforton. Male, 54lb, length 52in, girth 28in, two years river-life and four years feeding in the sea, a typical very large spring fish which had not spawned before; evidently a good shaped fish for its C.F. is 38½. As far as I know this is the second largest salmon caught by rod in the Wye during the last thirty years. The largest weighed 59½lb and was caught by Miss Davey in 1923. The following salmon weighing 50lb and over were caught by rod in the Wye since 1913:

1914	51lb	1930	50lb
1920	52lb	1930	50½lb
1923	59½lb	1931	50lb
1925	50lb	1935	50lb
1928	52½lb	1939	54lb

I give below particulars of all the Wye 50-pounders of which I have received scales:

	Date	Wt	Lth	Gth	C.F.	How Caught
1913	May 28	51½	51	26½	39	Nets
1913	June 9	51½	48½	28½	46	Nets
1914	March 20	51	49	29	43	Rod
1914	May 24	52	51	26½	39	Found dead
1915	May 21	52½	49	28½	44½	Nets
1920	March 21	52	54	26	33	Rod
1923	March 31	59½	52½	29	41	Rod
1928	April 4	52½	52½	28½	36½	Rod
1930	April 17	50	49	27	42½	Rod
1935	March 19	50	51	26½	38	Rod
1939	March 15	54	52	28	38½	Rod

Every one of these salmon was a cock fish and had spent two years in the river and four years feeding in the sea.

Yours sincerely
J. A. HUTTON

Mr William Fletcher (Mona)

1 Although female salmon of 50lb or more are rare, their gonads are also fully primed.
2 The salmon were nearly all caught where the rivers run into the lough. Each fish tends to nose its natal stream soon after running into the lough. Indeed, Spencer postulated that salmon needed to 'touch base' before dispersing throughout the lough – until a winter flood drew them to the spawning beds.

Appendix 4
SALMON-FARM ACTIVITY

In the first volume of *Giant Salmon*, on page 13, I wrote: 'While I was reading, or more precisely re-reading, the big-fish accounts, I was surprised to discover how young the salmon – approximately 98 per cent of which are cock fish – were at the time of capture.'

J. Arthur Hutton, a revered expert who spent a lifetime 'reading' the fish scales of many hundreds of salmon in order to ascertain the age of each fish, by calculating its early life in freshwater (two to three years) and its subsequent life at sea (one to five years), wrote in *Wye Salmon and Other Fish* (1949):

> People when they see a really big salmon, say of 40 or 50lb, would naturally think that it was a comparatively old fish, whereas as a matter of fact, it would probably be not more than five or six years old. The salmon is a rapid-growing but comparatively short-lived animal.

Hutton's conclusions, so far as British rivers are concerned, are broadly accepted; but modern research has revealed that specific rivers, such as the Tana, which flows between Norway and Finland within the Arctic Circle, have strains of salmon that are much longer lived (up to 17 years). These fish have different spawning strategies. In other rivers, the inability of a salmon to survive the spawning act, particularly male fish, is wrapped in mystery. Why should nearly all male salmon running in most rivers die after spawning, whereas in northern Scandinavia some individuals survive up to three spawning acts?

That death is not the automatic fate for male Atlantic salmon following the spawning act, as it is with both sexes of the Pacific sockeye salmon (*Oncorhynchus nerka*), is evident when we study the results of experiments conducted by the research station on the River Almond, funded by the Tay Fisheries Board. Here both male and female fish can be induced to start feeding again soon after being stripped of their spawn and milt, and as a consequence rebuild weight in readiness for a repeat spawning act a year later. Indeed, one hen fish has survived a sequence of four spawning acts. Doubtless, such experiments with the Atlantic salmon are taking place in hatcheries in a number of countries.

The subject of rearing Atlantic salmon for the table tends to make caring salmon fishermen somewhat uneasy, perhaps because it tends to remind them of the potential of fish farming to harm the runs of wild salmon. I imagine that most of the worriers believe that the people who run the farms collect their breeding stock annually by netting salmon rivers and stripping wild stock. In fact, in the 1970s, the Norwegian salmon fishing industry, realizing that the wild population could no longer sustain commercial salmon fishing, changed its fundamental approach. Instead of using wild fish for brood stock, they adopted a breeding programme similar to the one that had been used in agriculture for thousands of years – they used brood stock derived from their wild counterparts, but separated by thirty or more generations – although some netting of wild fish for the market is still practised and some wild fish are still used for brood stock.

Norway has led the way in establishing breeding programmes, starting in the late 1960s, and has produced four named strains of salmon, for example the Mowie strain, and another based on fish samples from forty Norwegian rivers and one Swedish river. Much more information on this subject can be found in *The Atlantic Salmon* by Verspoor, Stradmeyer and Nielsen.

After reading a copy of the *Fishing Gazette* dated 31 July 1909, I realized that a hundred years ago the Edwardians were already privy to this information about keeping mature salmon in freshwater tanks:.

The Scottish Fishery Board's Report

A very useful feature of the twenty-seventh annual report of the Fishery Board for Scotland is an Index to matters in the report for 1892–1907.

A Salmon Kept Alive Twelve Months Without Food

The most interesting thing in the report is a portrait and account of a male kelt salmon which was kept for a whole year in a place where it could get no food. Professor Noel Paton, who examined the fish for Mr Calderwood, said that the fish was extraordinarily poor in fat. The fish had 12 months previously been stripped of its milt for fertilising salmon eggs (it was only a small fish, 5lb) and had been kept all the year in a space 6ft by 12ft, with only about a foot of water in it. Yet in captivity and for 12 months without food its milt had again ripened and was successfully used for impregnating ova before it was killed. The photograph does not give that impression of emaciation which one would expect from so long a fast and enforced absence from salt-water. The moral is an eye-opener for those who think that salmon cannot live even 6 months in fresh-water without feeding.

Calderwood's discovery brought a response from the exceedingly clear-thinking correspondent 'Mona' (nom de plume of William Fletcher, see Appendix 3), which was published in the *Fishing Gazette* on 7 August 1909. As the letter shows, Mona anticipated by at least half a century the research funded by the Tay Fisheries Board concerned with kelt salmon feeding in freshwater.

STARVING SALMON

DEAR SIR – Mr Calderwood's experiment with his imprisoned salmon was exceedingly interesting, but cannot, I fear, be considered quite conclusive, and certainly will not silence the Philistines. That salmon can stand long fasts in fresh water, possibly extending to quite twelve months, or even more, has long been almost common knowledge, but what we want to know is, would they take food if the opportunity offered. Mr Calderwood should kindly try again, and imprison another fish, and when a few months have passed try him with prawns, worms, small fish, and the like, living and dead, and then we shall see what we shall see. That a salmon may seize a moving object in the water we all know, or even pick up worms and shrimps in conditions where these latter can scarcely be said to be moving, but feeding means more than all this. The salmon must fairly and squarely digest his food, or his 'feeding' is a mere abortive thing signifying nothing more than an acute attack of gastritis dementia of some sort. Feeding to be acknowledged as such must be effective, and it is not enough to know salmon take food, as they certainly do take, or seem to take, shrimps and worms upon occasion. We also want to know what they do with it when they take it, and to this end this second experiment is respectfully suggested.

Yours truly,

MONA

Appendix 5
LARGE WYE SALMON

Although the River Wye is famous for its big salmon, which are usually and uniquely referred to in angling reports and literature as portmanteaux fish, it is sobering to look at the odds against an individual catching one. In H.A. Gilbert's *The Tale of a Wye Fisherman* (Jonathan Cape, 1928, reprinted with revisions, 1953) we read:

> Mr. Morland, of Foy, the well-known Wye fisherman, has sent me particulars of 1531 salmon, which he has killed in the last thirty years. He began to fish in 1896 during the netting times and, curious to relate, the very first salmon he hooked was a real 'portmanteau'. This fish took Mr. Morland's minnow in the Carrots, and broke the trace. A fortnight later the netsman very politely handed him back his tackle with the tantalizing information that the fish out of whose mouth they had obtained it weighed forty-three pounds. Mr. Morland had to fish the Wye for another seventeen years before he caught a fish of over forty pounds, and after that again he had to fish for fifteen years more before he caught a second.

On page 135 of the 1953 reprint, Gilbert lists all of the Wye salmon weighing 50lb or more.

	Year	Weight lbs	Angler	Water
1	1914	51	J. Wyndham Smith	Aramstone
2	1920	52	Col. Tilney	Higgins Wood
3	1923	59½	Miss Davy (Mrs. Pryce Jenkin)	Cowpond
4	1925	50		Courtfield
5	1928	52½	The late Hon. R. Devereux	The Nyth
6	1930	50	Sir Thomas Merton	Castleton
7	1930	50½	Col. Heywood	Caradoc
8	1931	50		Stowfield at Lidbrook
9	1935	50	Captain Yates	Ballingham
10	1937	50½		Rocklands
11	1939	54	Sir Thomas Merton	Cowpond

Gilbert stated: 'The above fish were all caught on bait. Fish over 40 pounds have rarely been caught on fly,' but perhaps he was wrong about Devereux's fish. See page 235 of *Giant Salmon* for conflicting evidence.

Appendix 6
THE LARGEST ICELANDIC SALMON – 54lb

This fine cast of a ten-year-old Grímsey salmon is 52in long – longer than one would expect for its weight. According to Sturdy's table, it should weigh between 56½ and 60½lb but I daresay that the weight, given as 24.5kg bled, means that it weighed 54lb after being eviscerated.

In August 2008 I received a letter from fish and fisheries biologist Dr Derek Mills. It provided me with the essential details of a 97lb Icelandic salmon caught near Grímsey, an island north of Iceland, together with an intriguing catch account and a photograph of the fish, published in the Icelandic newspaper *Morgunbladid*, on Friday, 1 April 1960. Dr Mills, sceptical when he noticed the date of the newspaper, made a few enquiries and was not surprised to find that the weight claim was a hoax.

Making those subsequent enquiries, however, turned out to be a blessing because his correspondent, Árni Isaksson, head of salmonid management at the Icelandic Directorate of Fisheries, told him that a large salmon had indeed been landed, and gave details of what is probably an all-time record for an Icelandic-caught fish (it may have been destined to run up a river in another country). It weighed 54lb and to confirm its authenticity, Árni Isaksson wrote:

I can assure you that the [54lb] salmon caught off Grímsey was not an

April fools thing as I have it mounted on a wall in my organization. Salmon caught in Icelandic angling have, however, never been this big and I believe that they have never exceeded 40 pounds. Judging from scale samples and tagging experiments Icelandic salmon are rarely more than 2SW* and do thus not reach a phenomenal size. The salmon off Grímsey was caught in 1957, over 10 years old, 132cm fork length and 24.5kg bled. It had only spawned once and was thus feeding in the sea for a long time. We don't really know either whether it was of Icelandic origin.

Referring to the huge increase of salmon in Icelandic waters, especially those that have spent two winters at sea, he wrote:

Turning to other issues, we have had a phenomenally good salmon season this year with a considerable recovery of 2SW salmon, which have been low for a number of years. Whether this means that we see an increase in abundance in Greenland remains to be seen. The total Icelandic catch will probably be record high, exceeding 60,000 salmon.

Appendix 7
ROBERT STRAWBRIDGE'S 50lb 12oz ALTEN RIVER SALMON

On 28 August 2005, Robert Strawbridge of Wyoming caught a salmon estimated to weigh 50¾lb in the Ovre Sierra pool on Norway's Alten River. He was using a Willie Gunn tube fly that he had purchased from Farlows in London. Although the salmon, a cock fish, was returned alive, from the measurements taken Ellen McCaleb was able to make an excellent carving of the fish. From the description, she was also able to paint it to show the salmon's unusual colour.

---

* 2SW salmon are those that have spent two winters at sea, rather than grilse, which have been at sea fro one winter.

Ellen McCaleb, the woodcarver from Barrington, New Hampshire, posing with her carving of Robert Strawbridge's big fish – it was tempting, out of respect for the fish, to print the photograph horizontally rather than vertically.

Appendix 8
A RECORD FISH FROM THE NESS?

In October 2007 the news of the well-witnessed capture of a very large cock salmon from a deep pool in Scotland's River Ness leaked out to the media. The fish was measured, photographed and returned alive, without being weighed, because no suitable scales were to hand. Despite the presence of four witnesses, there was considerable confusion concerning the measurements of its length and girth, with the result that it has been distressingly difficult even to guess the weight of this fish.

Judging from R. Bremner's photograph, from the various lengths quoted I would certainly choose 56in as the likeliest one, but I am afraid that the quoted girth measurement of 50in is almost certainly incorrect.

Appendix 9
JOHN RENNIE AND THE DESTRUCTION OF THE SHANNON

In 1929 the Electricity Supply Board completed the Shannon Power Scheme. Lough Derg had been extended from Killaloe a further 4 miles downstream, where it was met by the great dam and headworks at Parteen, which considerably reduced the volume of the flow of the old river. All of this changed the historic nature of the old river to which its population of salmon had long since adapted.

In fairness it must be said that the authorities had built an excellent fish-pass that allowed running salmon easy access to the rest of the river system but, sadly, the changes ruined the nature of the holding water below Castleconnell, where the famous beats of World's End, Summerfield, New Garden, Doonass, Hermitage, Prospect and Woodlands are huddled along both banks of the river. These beats provided most if not all of the giant Shannon salmon (twelve) featured in this book.

The vastly experienced salmon fisherman John Rennie, sometime member of the Flyfishers' Club, wrote a chapter on the River Shannon for *Salmon Fishing*, published by Seeley Service (volume 10 in the Lonsdale Library Series, 1931). He had this to say about fishing at Castleconnell:

You must picture to yourself a great, broad, rugged river, tumbling through locks and opening out into great pools.

There may be larger rivers; but the Shannon at Castleconnell is the most sporting bit of river I know.

I remember, after I had been broken or cut by two or three fish, my boatman said, 'But you see, your honour, they are built for speed and power,' and so they are.

Rennie then tried to explain why the fishing had deteriorated so dramatically:

What is left of the Shannon?

Not much it is true; but we must make the best of what there is left. While we are thinking about this run of fish through Castleconnell, the following observation might be made. In the old days it was said, and I think rightly, that the large fish did not appear to go above the sluices at Killaloe, and the old fishermen would tell you that they slacked back to the spawning beds below Castleconnell. This opinion appears to be well founded as hardly any fish were seen or caught above Killaloe, there may have been a few; but I am speaking generally.

Now let us see what is happening. Since the salmon pass has been made at Porteen Villa, the fish have been romping up, big and small in great numbers. What they will do when they find themselves in a big strange lake, remains to be seen. I doubt if they will return and go down the river again to spawn, and if not, they will have to find other spawning grounds higher up the lakes.

Appendix 10
SOME YOU WIN AND SOME YOU LOSE

On page 136 of *Giant Salmon*, mention is made of a 55lb salmon that Colonel William Bromley-Davenport, later Sir William, caught on fly on Norway's Rauma River. An account of his battle to land this fish is generally considered to be the best description of man versus salmon that has ever been published. It first appeared in *Sport* (Chapman & Hall, 1885) and was reprinted in full, some ten pages, in Oglesby and Money-Coutts' book *The Big Fish* (Robinson, 1992).

A second piece by Davenport was also included in *Sport*, which was reprinted four times (the last one by Maclehose & Co, 1933). This details another epic battle on the same river, which resulted in the loss of a much bigger fish. Davenport's description of his growing expectations, in the certain knowledge that the fish he was playing weighed over 60lb, followed by his crushing disappointment three hours later when the hook fell out as the beaten fish lay on its side, is easily the most compelling account I have ever read.

> Five o'clock P.M. – we have eaten the best portion of a Norwegian sheep, not much bigger than a good hare, for our dinner, and the lower water awaits us. Here the valley is wider, the pools larger and less violent. It is here that I have always wished to hook the real monster of the river – the sixty or seventy-pounder of tradition as I can follow him to the sea if he don't yield sooner, which from the upper water I can't, because impossible rapids divide my upper and lower water; and if I had not killed this morning's fish where I did I should have lost him, as it was the last pool above the rapids. We take ship again in Nedre Fiva, a splendid pool, about a mile from my house, subject only to the objection which old Sir Hyde Parker, one of the early inventors of Norway fishing, used to bring against the whole country: "Too much water and too few fish!" I have great faith in myself today, and feel that great things are still in store for me. I recommence operations, and with some success, for I land a twelve and a sixteen pounder in a very short space of time; after which, towards the tail of this great pool, I hook something very heavy and strong, which runs out my line in one rush almost to the last turn of the reel before Ole can get way on the boat to follow him, and then springs out of the water a full yard high; this feat being performed some 120 yards off me, and the fish looking even at that distance enormous. I have no doubt that I have at last got fast to my ideal monster – the

seventy-pounder of my dreams. Even the apathetic Ole grunts loudly his 'Gud bevarr!' of astonishment. I will spare the reader all the details of the struggle which ensues, and take him at once to the final scene, some two miles down below where I hooked him, and which has taken me about three hours to reach – a still back-water, into which I have with extraordinary luck contrived to guide him, dead-beat. No question now about his size. We see him plainly close to us, a very porpoise. I can see that Ole is demoralised and unnerved at the sight of him. He had twice told me, during our long fight with him, that the forty-three pounder of this morning was 'like a small piece of this one' – the largest salmon he had ever seen in his fifty years' experience; and to my horror I see him, after utterly neglecting one or two splendid chances, making hurried and feeble pokes at him with the gaff with the only effect of frightening him by splashing the water about his nose.

In a fever of agony I bring him once again within easy reach of the gaff, and regard him as my own. He is mine now! He must be! 'Now's your time, Ole can't miss him! Now – now!' He does though, and in one instant a deadly sickness comes over me as the rod springs straight again, and the fly dangles useless in the air. The hold has broken. Still the fish is so beat that he lies there yet on his side. He knows not he is free! 'Quick, gaff him as he lies. Quick! Do you hear? You can have him still!' Oh, for a Scotch gillie! Alas for the Norwegian immovable nature! Ole looks up at me with lack-lustre eyes, turns an enormous quid in his cheek, and does nothing. I cast down the useless rod, and dashing at him wrest the gaff from his hand, but it is too late. The huge fins begin to move gently, like a steamer's first motion of her paddles, and he disappears slowly into the deep! Yes – yes, he is gone! For a moment I glare at Ole with a bitter hatred. I should like to slay him where he stands, but have no weapon handy, and also doubt how far Norwegian law would justify the proceeding, great as is the provocation. But the fit passes, and a sorrow too deep for words gains possession of me, and I throw away the gaff and sit down, gazing in blank despair at the water. Is it possible? Is it not a hideous nightmare? But two minutes ago blessed beyond the lot of angling man – on the topmost pinnacle of angling fame! The practical possessor of the largest salmon ever taken with a rod! And now, deeper than ever plummet sounded, in the depths of dejection! Tears might relieve me; but my sorrow is too great, and I am doubtful how Ole might take it. I look at him again. The same utterly blank face, save a projection of unusual size in his cheek, which makes me conjecture that an additional quid has been secretly thrust in to supplement the one already in possession. He has said not a word since the catastrophe, but abundant expectoration testifies to the deep and tumultuous workings of his soul. I bear in mind that I am a man and a Christian, and I mutely offer him my flask. But, no; with a delicacy which does him honour, and touches me to the heart, he declines it; and with a deep sigh and in scarcely audible accents repeating, 'The largest salmon I ever saw in my life!', picks up my rod and prepares to depart. Why am I not a Stoic, and treat this incident with contempt? Yes; but why am I human? Do what I will, the vision is still before my eyes. I hear the 'never, never can the chance recur again!' Shut my eyes, stop my ears as I will, it is the same. If I had only known his actual weight! Had he but consented to be weighed and returned into the stream! How gladly would I now make that bargain with him! But the opportunity of even that compromise is past. It's intolerable. I don't believe the Stoics ever existed; if they did they must have suffered more than even I do in bottling up their miseries. They did feel; they must have felt – why pretend they didn't? Zeno was a humbug! Anyhow, none of the sect ever lost a salmon like that! What! 'A small sorrow? Only a fish!' Ah, try it yourself! An old lady, inconsolable for the loss of her dog, was once referred for example of resignation to a mother who had lost her child, and she replied, 'Oh, yes, *but children are not dogs!*' And I, in some sort, understand her. So, in silent gloom, I follow Ole homewards.

Not darkness, nor twilight, but the solemn yellow hues of northern midnight gather over the scene; black and forbidding frown the precipices on either side, save where on the top of the awful Horn – inaccessible as happiness – far, far beyond the reach of mortal footstep, still glows, like sacred fire, the sleepless sun! Hoarser murmurs seem to arise from the depths of the foss, like the groans of imprisoned demons, to which a slight but increasing wind stealing up the valley from the sea adds its melancholy note. My mind, already deeply depressed, yields helplessly to the influence of the hour and sinks to zero at once; and despondency – the hated spirit – descends from her "foggy cloud" and is my inseparable companion all the way home.

Appendix 11
MORE ABOUT THE LARGEST TWEED SALMON – 70lb?

On pages 422–24 of *Giant Salmon*, I told the story of a fish that was hooked and lost by one of the lairds of Bemersyde and described by Sir Herbert Maxwell in his book *Great Hours in Sport* (1921). In 2006, while I was investigating the locations of big-fish stories, I managed to interview the then Earl Haig, the 30th Laird of Bemersyde. As a result of this pleasant encounter, I was able to add a few more facts to the story told by Sir Herbert Maxwell; but it was still unclear when the incident took place.

In January 2009 I received a letter from Earl Haig, who sadly died on 10 July that year. He had read the book and pointed out that in fact it was not his father, Field Marshal Sir Douglas Haig, the 29th Laird of Bemersyde, who had hooked and lost the mighty fish, but the 28th Laird back in 1883. This is what he wrote:

> I am writing as the person you met when you came here some years ago to survey the Tweed beat where a large fish was lost by my late cousin Colonel Arthur Haig. I enclose a copy of his fishing diary for August 29th 1883. Your book reports the angler was my father and you may have misheard what I told you. Arthur Balfour Haig was the 28th Laird. Later in 1921 Bemersyde was purchased in a sale by friends and admirers of my father and was presented to him when he became 29th Laird. My father died in 1928, too young at 67 years, and later in the 1950s, I was made chief of the Haigs by the then Lord Lyon. I had become the 30th Laird on the death of my father.
>
> There will be an article in *Salmon & Trout* in about 2 or 3 months about Bemersyde – my father's time as Laird will be described as also my own.

The original entry made by Colonel Arthur Balfour Haig (see below) interestingly sheds light on a number of cloudy issues. We now know that the fish was hooked and lost on 29 November 1883, and that the leading poacher was a Mr Paterson. Curiously, there is no mention of the fish having been cut in two, but if it was cut in two for the convenience of putting it into a sack, the parts must have been weighed together in order for the four poachers to assert a weight of 64lb.

This is the extract from Arthur Balfour Haig's fishing diary for 1883:

THE MONSTER SALMON I LOST

On the 29th November I hooked a salmon in the Pool [The Cradle Pool] in the afternoon. He ran me down to below Jock Sure [the next pool downstream] close to the Monk's Ford – Moody and the under fisherman were both with me. At Monk's Ford, after nearly an hour's play the fish was tired out and the under fisherman went into the water to net him – he had the fish's head three times in the net, but each time it slipped out again – the

man said the net would hold only the fish's head and that it was hopeless to try to get him into the net. After the third try the gut broke and the fish escaped. I heard afterwards that a noted poacher called Paterson assisted by three others got this fish out the following night and they asserted that the weight was 64lb.
Signed by Colonel Arthur Balfour Haig 28th Laird of Bemersyde and copied from his Fishing Book by Haig of Bemersyde, 30th Laird (son of F.M.)

In my reply to Earl Haig on 5 January 2009, I wrote:

It was very kind of you to put me straight on the matter of which member of your family lost the big fish. When the time comes for a second volume of the book to be published, I intend to extend the entry to include the corrections. To this end, I have enclosed a rough draft for your approval.

After receiving the following reply, dated 8 January 2009, I believe that this story, which nearly anticipated Georgina Ballantine's record catch by 39 years, can be put to bed with a measure of confidence:

Dear Mr Buller,

Many thanks for your letter about the Fishing Book and the entry of the fish that got away. I am glad you have put a good entry for the fish for the purposes of your book and please go ahead with the correct words.

With kind regards,
Haig

Appendix 12
'DINNAS' IN SALMON FISHING

On the 28 June 1931, *The Field* published a truly valuable piece with the above title, purporting to be the acquired wisdom of a gillie's lifetime experience on Scotland's River Naver. I have taken the (justifiable?) liberty of substituting the word 'gaff' with 'net' because the gaff has now all but disappeared from the angling scene.

Dinna go out without going over this list: rod, reel, flies, casts, net, fish mat, lunch, whisky.

Dinna be sure of a big day's catch even though the river is at the right height, wind right, clouds right. There may be no fish on your beat! Sometimes the most unlikely day will bring the big catch.

Dinna use big flies to start with – many a fish is lost by using too big a fly. Use the big size later. A big fly may rise him; then use a small fly over him.

Dinna pull till the fish pulls you. If you pull the fly from him when he rises, he will not come again; better not to touch him than that.

Dinna use a longer line than you can get out straight; a short line straight is better than a long line crooked.

Dinna net your fish till he is coming in on his side with the eye out of the water. He does not see when his eye is out of the water.

Dinna forget always to stand opposite your fish when playing him. You will kill him in half the time; if he is below you, he is resting on your line; if he is above you, you are pulling the fly back from the way it went in. A fish always keeps as near the bottom as possible when being played until he gets tired. When he wriggles on the surface, put the point of the rod down above him so as to put the line as much under water as possible to keep his head under water. When he jumps, drop the rod point so as to slacken the line; many a fish is lost if the line is tight in the jump.

Work the Fly by Hand, not by Rod

Dinna forget always to draw your line in by your hand according to the run of the water; keep it moving quickly with very slow movement of the point. By working the rod and not drawing the line, the fly is only moving up and down, whereas it should be coming two feet at a draw up the stream. A fish will then make a proper nip at the fly as it will think it is to lose it; whereas the other way it will follow it round and get a good look at it and probably just touch it when you are going to make the cast.

Dinna use a lot of flies; time is lost in changing. Three flies a day is plenty. For instance, fishing the Naver in April and May, should you be reduced to taking three flies, they would be Popham, Greenwell and Childers. The nearer the sea, the less particular are the fish.

Dinna expect but you will get disappointed if the wind is in the east, as many a fish is lost when the east wind blows. They come short.

Dinna use the same fly as the party who was getting fish the day before on the same water. I have known of five fish being got on a Greenwell, and the angler fishing the same water next day with the same sort of weather could not move a fish until he changed to a Jock Scott, and then got fish, five on the same pools he fished with the Greenwell.

Dinna be downhearted if you lose a fish – that fish was not meant for you. Dinna forget that after weighing the fish, the flask must be produced – 'salmon and whisky go together'.

Dinna eat too much dinner, or you will dream of the fish you lost.
Dinna drink too much whisky, or your 'hope' will be too great for tomorrow.

Alick McHardy

BIBLIOGRAPHY

TITLE	AUTHOR	PUBLISHER	DATE
The Art of Angling (fourth edition)	Richard Brookes	W. Lowndes, London	1774
The Angler's Guide	T.F. Salter	T. Tegg, London	1815
The Angler's Companion to the Rivers and Lochs of Scotland	Thomas Tod Stoddart	William Blackwood and Sons	1853
Sport	Sir William Bromley-Davenport	Chapman & Hall, London	1885
Fishing Salmon & Trout	Henry Cholmondeley-Pennell	Badminton Library	1885
The Restigouche and its Salmon Fishing	Dean Sage	David Douglas, Edinburgh	1888
The Salmon	A.E. Gathorne-Hardy	Longmans, Green and Co., London	1898
Fishing	Captain C. Radcliffe	Country Life	1904
Life History and Habits of the Salmon, Sea Trout, Trout and Other Freshwater Fish	P.D. Malloch	A & C Black	1910
A History of Fly Fishing for Trout	John Waller Hills	Philip Allan, London	1921
Where the Spring Salmon Run	Patrick R. Chalmers	Philip Allan, London	1931
Sport	Sir William Bromley-Davenport	Maclehose & Co., London	1933
My Sporting Life	John Waller Hills	Philip Allan, London	1936
The Life of the Salmon	W.L. Calderwood	Edward Arnold, London	1938
Casts from a Salmon Reel	Major Kenneth Dawson	Herbert Jenkins, London	1948
The Tale of a Wye Fisherman	H.A. Gilbert	Jonathan Cape, London	1953
Pike Fishing	Norman L. Weatherall	Witherby, London	1961
Out of the Mainstream	Philip Kingsland Crowe	Charles Scribner's Sons, New York	1970
Scotland's King of Fish	Derek Mills	William Blackwood & Sons, Edinburgh	1980
So We Fished on the Lower Rhine	Werner Bocking	Kleve Boss	1989
This Fishing Life	Bob Church	Crowood Press	2003
The Grand Cascapedia River	Hoagy B. Carmichael	Meadow Run Press	2006
Saving Scotland's Salmon	Derek Mills	Medlar Press	2009

PHOTOGRAPHIC CREDITS

Fred Buller would like to thank, in particular, Morten Harangen for undertaking the unenviable task of locating Fridgeir Sagmo's descendents and, having found them, successfully seeking their permission for him to publish the photograph on page 108. His thanks to Sagmo's daughter are as unquestioning as was her gift of the photograph to a stranger.

Hewould also like to acknowledge a debt to the NationalMuseums of Scotland for prints of four watercolours (on pages 12, 18, 22 and 184) by the Scottish artist J.F. Campbell, all of which were executed circa 1850. These images reflect the activity of early British exploitation of Norwegian salmon fishing. The paintings were brought to his attention by Dr Roy Flury.

All illustrations are copyright the author, with the following exceptions, which are kindly provided by the individuals or institutions listed below.

Alfred Pope 159; Algernon Perrey 135; Alisdair Kirk 189; The Alta Association 48; *Altenposten* 2; Anthony Desbruslais 121; from Augustus Grimble, *The Salmon Rivers of Ireland* (Kegan Paul, Trench, Trübner, & Co. Ltd, London, 1913) 26, 128, 151; from Augustus Grimble, *The Salmon Rivers of Scotland* (Kegan Paul, Trench, Trübner, & Co. Ltd, London) 128; Bruce Latimer 105; Charles Kewley of Bonhams 148; Christian Bjelland 118; David Hatwell 6, 145; David Hatwell/LA84 Foundation 41; Dr Derek Mills 215; Douglas Evans 146; Sir Edward Dashwood Bt 113; Espen Ørud 63; *Fish&Fly* online magazine/Overalla Hotel, Grong 198; Graeme Davidson 38; James Greenwood 49; Jeremy Bloch 79; Joan Dugdale 130; Keith Elliott 132; Leif Inge Andersen 119; Malcolm Greenhalgh 44; Morten Harangen 81; Morton Seaman 53; National Library of Scotland 12, 18, 22, 184; National Museums Scotland 99; Øyvind Myran 94; from P.D. Malloch, *Life History and Habits of the Salmon Sea-Trout and Other Freshwater Fish* (Adam and Charles Black, London, 1910) 96; Reverend Nigel Pearson 89; Roger Hughes 33, 35; Roy Flury 122; Runi Østiyngen 51; from *Salmon*, (Edward Arnold, London) 163; from *So We Fished the Lower Rhine* (Kleve Boss, Kleve); from *This Fishing Life* (Crowood Press, Ramsbury Marlborough) 62; Tore Tiltnes 73; Tormod Nielsen 43; Vidar Kristensen/*Alta Post* 82; Warrington Archives 67; www.finmarkdagbled.no 80; www.silverrunpublishing.worldpress.com 195.

The author and publishers have endeavoured to trace the copyright holders, where necessary, for the images reproduced. This has not been possible in all cases and they apologize for any unwitting infringement of copyright.

INDEX

Page numbers in *italics* refer to illustrations.

A
Allen, Thomas 100
Alta River *see* Alten River
Altaposten 80, 82, 122, 194–6
Alten Fjord 80lb salmon 122
Alten River 8, *12*, *18*, *22*, *48*, 122, *122*, 184, 194–6, *195*
    salmon between 50lb–60lb (fly-caught) 40, *40*, 43, *43*, 45–7, *46*, 48, *48*, 49–50, *49*, 51, 52, 54, 56, *56*, 57–9, *58*, 65, *65*, 69–70, *69*, 76–7, *77*, 78–9, *79*, 80, *80*, 82–3, *82*, 189–90, *189*, 216, 217
Angling 66, 90, 203–4
Antonsen, Einar 68
Ardersier fishing community 98, *99*
Arnesen, Svein Ole 189
Ashley-Cooper, John 11
Astley, J. W. 147–8
Atlantic Salmon Journal 138
Avon River (Hampshire) 93

B
bag (lave) netting 113, 118
Bainbridge, G. B. 143–4, *143*
Balbach, Charles 57–9
Ballantine, Georgina 171, *172*, 173–7, *176*, *177*, *178*
Bårdsen, Egil Olai 122
Bardu River 71–4, *73*
Beauly River 94
Bervie Bay 37–9, *38*
Berners, Dame Juliana 8
Bjelland, Christian 112
Bjøra River 181
Blackwater River 88
Blinker 83
Bloch, Jeremy 78–9, *79*
Blois, Sir Charles 91–2
Bocking, Werner 110
Border Esk River 60lb salmon 62–5, *64*
Bradley Martin, Esmond 138–41, *139*
Bromley-Davenport, Sir William 220–2
Brookes, Richard 66
Buckland, Frank 93, 115, 200, 202
Burness, Provost John 37, *37*, 39

C
Canada 41 *see also* Grand Cascapedia River
Carmichael, Hoagy. B. 41
Carroll, Charles 150–2
Chalmers, Patrick E. 74–75
Chanonry Point 98, *99*
Cheyne, Charles 116
Cholmondeley-Pennell, H. 179–80
Church, Bob 62
Clarke, David 48, *48*
Cooper, Tony 189–90
Corabber River 208
Corbett, E.M. 162, *163*
Corbett, Edward 208, *209*
Coxen, Richard 114, 115, 205
Craven, W. G. 134, *134*
Crosby, Alan 67
Cunard, Major 55

D
Daily Mail 38
Dalsegg, John H. 81, *81*
Daniloff, Ernst 80, *80*
Darling, William 96
Dashwood, Sir Edward 118
Davey, Miss 168–70
Davidson, Mr W. 134, *135*
Dawson, Major Kenneth 157–8
de Burgh, Clare 57
Dee River 90, 121
Deterding, Shirley 43–5, *43*
Devereux, Mr R.G. 138, *139*, 152, 215
Dominick, Peter 57–9
Dønheim, Peder A. 81
Doonass (*Fishing Gazette* writer) 150–7
Drummond, Dr W.H. 41
Dunn, J.W. 41

E
Eden River 105
Eids River 60lb salmon 101
Eira River 144
Elliot, John 103
Em River 83
Emaus, Jørgen *48*
England *see* Avon River (Hampshire); Border Esk River; Eden River; Mersey River; Severn River; Thames River; Wye River
Eriboll, Loch 127
Evanger River 162
Ewe River *128*, 131

F
Falkner, Thomas 115–16
farming fish *see* fish-farming
Faroese 70lb salmon 112, *113*
Farrer, Joyce 86, *86*, *87*
Farrer, Trevor 86, 147–8
Ffennell, Henry 105–6, 111, 115, 131–2, 136, 200, 201–2, 205–6
The Field 200, 226–7
Firth of Forth 60lb salmon 109, *109*
fish-farming 211–13
Fishing Gazette 88, 100, 102, 105–6, 114–15, 117, 131–2, 151, 152, 153–7, 136, 168–70, 182–3, 200–1, 191–2, 212–23, 209, 151, 152–7
Fitzgerald, Mollie 69–70, *69*
Fletcher, William 'Mona' 206–7, *210*, 213
Ford, Liam 153
Francis, Francis 91–2, 114, *114*, 115, 117

G
Gabba, Tony 186–7
Garnett and Keegan 150–1
Germany *see* Rhine River
Gideon, Collie 138, *139*, 140–1
Gilbert, H.A. 209, 214–15
Golding, Terry 32, *33*, 34–6
Gore, Hugh 38
Grand Cascapedia River 41, 138, 140–1, 182–3, 190–4
Grant, Osgood *130*, 131, 132
Greenwood, James 49–50, *49*, 59
Grieg, Mr 119–20
Grímsey salmon 215–16
Grove's (fishmonger) 105, 182, 201, 205
Guest, Merthyr 166

H
Haig, Arthur Balfour 223–5
Hall, Samuel and Anna 115
Hamilton, Edward 204
Hammari, Thorieif 51, *51*
Hammersvik, Stian 40, *40*
Hampton, J.F. 203–4
Harangen, Morten 81, 106–8
Hardy, Eric 66–7, 90
harling 71–3, 173, 197
Harrison, Shawn 191–4
Hauge, Major Ivar 145
Hills, John Waller 71–4
Hjelle, Knut 102
Hjelle, Martin 101–2, *101*
Hoare, Sir David 45–7
Hodgkiss, David 34
Holten, Svein Lyon 189
Hope Estuary 109lb salmon 124–7
Hughes, Roger 32, 34
Hughes-Parry, Jack 146
Hutton, J. Arthur 168–9, 175, 207–8, 209–10, 211

I
Iceland 215–16
Inverness Advertiser 98
Ireland 208–9 *see also* Blackwater River; Screebe River; Shannon River
The Irish Field 207
Isaksson, Árni 215–16

J
Jacobsen, Kai 181, *181*
John Enright and Son 152
Johnstone, Andrew 103, *104*
Jørgen, Sverre *48*

K
Kemppainen, Heike 42, *42*
Kyrke, R. Venables 64

L
Latchford Causey 66–7
Latimer, Bruce 102–3
Lauth, Holger 83
Lea, Rupert 49–50, 59–60, *61*
Lindsay, Dr Alexander 146, *146*
Lithuania 123
London 115–16, 182–3 *see also* Thames River
London Globe 110
Lough Eske 208
Loweymore River 208

M
Maales River System 71–4, *73*
McCaleb, Ellen 216, *217*
Mackintosh, Alexander 67
Maclellan, Peter 75
MacMillan, John 56, *56*
Maher, Michael 136
Marston, R. B. 115
Mathieson, Rev. John 98
Maxwell, Sir Herbert 203, 204, 223
McDonnell, W. F. 150–7
McGuane, Thomas 86
McHardy, Alick 226–27
Mersey River 66–7, *67*
Milburn, Fred 136, *137*
Mills, Derek 112, 113
Mona (journalist) 206–7, *210*, 213
Montrose 105–6
Moray Firth 98, *99*
Morrum River 62
Mosesen, Karstein 58–59, *58*
Mosesen, Kjetl 78–9
Mosesen, Tormod 57–9, *58*, 78–9
Myran, Mr 94

N
Nagellhus, Tor Kjetil 197, *198*
Namsen River 92
 salmon (bait-caught) *188*, 188, 197, *198*
 salmon between 50lb–60lb (fly-caught) 91–2, 160
 salmon between 50lb–60lb (method uncertain) 88, 89, 166–7
 60lb salmon 106–8, *108*
Naver River 226–7
Nemen Estuary 100lb salmon 123
Ness River 98, 218
Ness, Jock 164–5
nets and netting 122, 124, 201, 202
 bag 'lave' nets 113, 118
 Tay River 200–1
Nicolaysen, Dagfinn 122
Nid River 94
Nilsen, Arnulf 82–3
Nilsen, Ulf-Arne Jungord 82–3, *82*
Nordahl, Hjørdis 188
North America 41
North Esk River 38, 74–5
Norway 10, 101–2, 212 *see also* Alten Fjord; Alten River; Bardu River; Bj¯ra River; Eids River; Eira River; Evanger River; Maales River System; Namsen River; Nidelva River; Orkla River; Rauma River; Repparfjord River; Sand River; Stryn River; Suldal River; Surna River; Tana River; Vefsen River; Vosso River

O
O'Brien, Donal C. 190–4, *191*
Olausen, Paul Kristian *43*
Onslow, Richard 76–7, *77*
Opgård, Katrine 194–6, *195*
Opgård, Tormod 196
Orkla River 42
Outing Magazine 41

P
Palmer, Brian 34, *35*, 36
Park, Mr A. 160
Parrish, Donald 186–7
Paulsen, Magnus 56
Pearson, Lt. Col. N. G. 88, 89, 166
photography 68, 53, 188
Pullar, Major Frank 132, 149

R
Radclyffe, Captain C. E. 64–5, 160
Radclyffe, Mrs E. 160
Rauma River 220
Rennie, John 151, 218–19
Repparfjord River 63
Rhine River 60lb salmon 110, *111*
Romsdal, Sverre J. 56

S
Sachs, T. R. 114–15
Sage, Dean 182–3
Sagmo, Fridgeir 106–8, *107*, *108*
Sagmo, Inge 107, *108*
Salter, T. F. 179, 180, 204–5
Sand River 70lb salmon 119–120, *119*
Scotland 11 *see also* Bervie Bay; Ewe River; Firth of Forth; Naver River; North Esk River; Spey River; Tay River; Tweed River
Scottish Fishery Board 212–13
Screebe River 38
Seaman, Morton 32, 52, 53, 54
Severn River 60lb salmon 100
Shannon River 136, *137*, 150–7, *151*, 218–19
Simensen, Trond and Frode 60
Sivertsen, Tor Johnny 63, *63*
Slattery, D. 153
Spey River 134
Spiller, Miss E. 160
St George, Howard 38
St John, Sir Walter 116
Storvatnet Lake 63
Strawbridge, Robert 216–7
Stryn River 101
Sturdy Scale 207
Suldal River 70lb salmon 112–3, 118
Surna River 81
Swanson, Ronald 74
Sweden *see also* Em River; Morram River
Swensen, Tolliev 120

T
Tana River 70lb salmon 145
Tarbutt, Percy 144
Tay Fisheries Board 211, 213
Tay River 182–3, 200, 201
 record salmon 171–5
 salmon between 50lb–60lb (fly-caught) 55, *55*, 132, *133*, 148–9, *148*, 164–5, *165*
Tenvik, Ragnor 197–8
Thames River 114–7, 179–80, *180*, 203–5
Thomassen, Willy 65, *65*
Thurso River 91, *91*
Towy River 146, *146*
Trout & Salmon 32, 109, 124, 164, 186–7
Tuohy, M. 153
Tweed River 38, 223–5
Twickenham 114–7

V
Vefsen River
 salmon between 50lb–60lb (fly-caught) 64–5
 salmon between 50lb–60lb (method uncertain) 86, *87*, 147–8, 157–8
Verne, Mrs Jules 196
Vosso River 162, 207
 salmon between 50lb and 60lb (fly-caught) 32, *33*, 34–6

W
Wales 90, 146, *146*
Wallace, Major C. W. 157–8
Ward, Lettice 132, *133*
Weatherall, Norman 176–7
weighing and weight tables 11, 205–10
Welsh Dee River 90
Weyerke, Dr Marcus 101, 102
Wheen family 142
Whymper, Sam 147
Willett, Lorney *139*
Williams, Mrs 'Saucy' 166–7
Williksen, Johan 107, *108*
Wye River 152, 158–9, *159*, 168–70, 186–7, *186*, 207–10, 214–5